KEY

1 Hope Cemetery
Corti Monument

2 Grave of Justin Morgan
Grave of Figure

3 Joseph Smith Memorial

4 Donohue Sea Caves

5 Indian Stones

6 Fireworks

7 Champ

8 Bread and Puppet Museum

9 Art, Rest Area

10 Aspet / Saint-Gaudens
Historic Site

11 Dowsers Labyrinth
(Danville)

Round Schoolhouse
(Brookline)

The Round Church
(Richmond)

12 Fenian Raids

OFF the LEASH

Subversive Journeys
Around Vermont

Helen Husher [signature]

THE COUNTRYMAN PRESS
WOODSTOCK, VERMONT

OFF the LEASH

Subversive Journeys
Around Vermont

Helen Husher

Library of Congress Cataloging-in-Publication Data

Husher, Helen, 1951–
        Off the leash : subversive journeys around Vermont /
Helen Husher.— 1st ed.
                p.   cm.
                ISBN 0-88150-427-0 (alk. paper)
                1. Vermont—Description and travel. 2. Vermont
Guidebooks. 3. Vermont—History, Local. 4. Husher, Helen,
1951– —Journeys—Vermont. I. Title.
F55.H871999
974.3—dc21   99-28796
                                          CIP

The text of this book is composed in Bodoni.
Jacket and text design by Susan McClellan
Jacket painting by Kathleen Kolb
Map composed by Brian Callanan,
copyright © 1999 The Countryman Press

Published by The Countryman Press
PO Box 748
Woodstock, VT 05091

Distributed by W. W. Norton & Company, Inc.
500 Fifth Avenue, New York, NY 10110

Printed in the United States
10 9 8 7 6 5 4 3 2

To Alice and Tony Pickman

Acknowledgments

NOBODY WRITES A BOOK ALONE, and the unindicted co-conspirator on this one was Vince Sondej, my friend, companion, and editor, who gave me the three things every writer needs: guidance, criticism, and a river of unearned affection. Appreciation is also tendered to Christina Ward, Barney Bloom, Alfred Perry, and John Sims, and to my teachers, Alex Gold, J. B. White, and Celia Millward.

Contents

Introduction   *13*

1. **TAKEN FOR GRANITE**   27
   An Afternoon in Hope Cemetery

2. **JUSTIN MORGAN HAD A LIFE**   37
   A Man and His Horse

3. **FACING WEST**   49
   The Joseph Smith Memorial

4. **URBAN GLACIATION**   63
   The Donohue Sea Caves

5. **INDIAN STONES**   79
   The Captivity of Susanna Johnson

6. **FIREWORKS**   91
   Reconstructing Randolph

7. TALES FROM THE CRYPTOZOOLOGISTS 109
   The Monster in the Lake

8. WHEAT PASTE AND RAGS 125
   The Bread and Puppet Theater

9. A VERY '70S THING TO DO 141
   Abstractions on the Interstate

10. THE DEMANDS OF HEAVEN 155
    Aspet and Augustus Saint-Gaudens

11. CIRCULAR REASONING 165
    Church, School, and Labyrinth

12. BORDER LANDS 179
    The Irish Invasion of Canada

   Notes and Selected Readings 197

OFF
the
LEASH

Introduction

TRAVEL BOOKS OCCUPY A WELL-WORN NICHE IN OUR
society, and there seem to be two kinds. The first
is full of listings and phone numbers and little explosions of bold type—a directory rather than a narrative.
The second is all narrative: We watch the writer progress
across the landscape, sometimes describing and sometimes ruminating. These two genres are in the same part of
the bookstore but not really together, as if they were quar-
relsome siblings that have to be kept apart, and perhaps
they do. Guides solve problems: where to stay, where to
eat, how to avoid getting lost, what to look at. Narratives
describe outcomes: where I stayed, what I ate, how I got
lost, and what I saw. You take one kind of book with you,
along with your maps; it gets dirty and curls on the dash-
board, and you write little notes in the back. The other
kind stays home with the dog.

This book is in the middle ground. I have a sloppy
and combinational temperament that insists I squash my
peas *in with* my mashed potatoes, and I have never felt

much enthusiasm for this travel guide–travel book division. Worse, I think this division is false. There is no particular trick to eating and sleeping, or in finding places where eating and sleeping occur; the trick—at least for me—is in finding my way toward the essentials, and in understanding what these essentials are trying to explain. The other trick to travel is holding on to my meager supply of money, and this is the deep conflict between travel and tourism. They occupy the same semantic ground, but they are not the same.

TRAVEL IS A SEARCH FOR NEWNESS, for something different, and for a kind of magic. We like confirmation that places are genuine and that new places have something to tell us; we like to glimpse the forces that have come down from the clouds, like big hands, and squeezed places into being. If this is not true, and if places are interchangeable, then there is no point in going anywhere at all. Yet much of the work of tourism is to separate us from those forces and to offer, instead, a prettified and often rather costly version of a given destination. Which, I hasten to add, is fine—this version is easy to locate and eminently digestible and often captures the easy and obvious metaphors. In Vermont, these metaphors are country stores, changing leaves, covered bridges, and prim white-clapboarded villages around a green. Toss in a ski lift and a little maple syrup, stir, and pour.

This concoction is pleasant, but it glides over the meddling and sometimes messy forces that got Vermont to where it is today. Metaphors do this—they are built to glide, to simplify, to offer shorthand. But the truth (or the devil or the deity), as we are often told, is in the details, the particulars of a place.

To a large degree this book is about those details. It's about things overlooked and perhaps undervalued because they do not fit comfortably into the larger frame. They are subversive, as this book is subversive, because they deflect our attention away from the metaphor and back to the specific. And as a travel book it may be even more dangerous than that. Used in a certain way, this book will keep you, in utter contentment, at home.

I know this sounds odd, and I do feel like a bit like the schoolchild who has kicked a ball through a window. *But wait! Wait! Let me explain!* Here, I offer stories about things in Vermont only because that is where they happen to be. Which, written like that, seems like an extraordinarily stupid thing to say, but sometimes stupid things also happen to be true. I believe that each township, each state, each county in America has at least a few of the unexpected, resonant, talkative places I have found here. We must merely learn to look for them, listen, and ask them the right questions. The genius of place is in *all* places, distributed through the ongoing magic of history. Finding it takes attitude, not an itinerary.

A FEW YEARS AGO I wangled an invitation to Utah. Before I went there, Utah presented itself to me as one of those square places; if I pictured it at all, I saw the cowboy country of my television youth, sort of dry and bony and full of places called Wild Horse Canyon and Rustlers Gulch. There, people possied up, galloped frantically in bunches, and shot harmlessly at each other from behind gray boulders. It even appeared in my mind's eye in grainy black and white, so durable was the Saturday-morning, out-West imagery.

The point of this adventure was to extract myself, at least for a long weekend, from a gloomy living arrangement; a secondary purpose was to go somewhere, anywhere, that did not require a hat and mittens. I was grinding several axes at once, so loudly that the roar of the airplane engines was nearly inaudible, and when I touched down in Salt Lake City I was a worried little knot, a problem to myself and others, and a helpless bundle of impulses. In short, I was the same neurally fried and unhappy mess you see in Howard Johnsons across the nation—the archetypal American on vacation.

I bring up this encounter with the desert because embedded in that trip was the seed that eventually grew into this collection of essays. Petulant, pained, bored, and approaching sedentary middle age, I could see trouble coming and felt powerless to stop it. I needed proof that life was not exclusively about money and velocity; I needed proof of wonder, proof that the world held legitimate surprise, not just interruptions. But I didn't know these things were the things I needed. I thought I needed a little change of scenery.

In an act of charity I was taken to Nine Mile Canyon to see the petroglyphs left by the Ute and Fremont Indians. Nine Mile Canyon is about forty miles long, which is a little confusing, and it offers up a tumbled, rocky, intimidating landscape in a canyon that gets steadily higher, drier, and deeper. It did not look like Saturday-morning out-West television. It looked like Mars. This worried me. I'd never seen a petroglyph and had no idea what to look for. So I just looked around, generically, and saw nothing at all.

"How big are these things?" I asked my travel companion, who also would be my companion to many of the places in this book.

Vince shrugged. "Beats me."

I consulted our flimsy newsprint map, picked up on the way, looked at the little numbered sites on it, and nursed a grudge that there were no corresponding little numbered signs on the dusty road. The only thing on the road was a drift of cattle, licking their noses and eating the spiky shrubbery. All around me was a tangled, rocky stillness and an aggressive, escalating silence. No signs, no rangers in ecru hats, no Petroglyph Quik Stop—I did not find any of this reassuring.

Suddenly: "There." It came out of my mouth before I

even knew what I was looking at—a spiral, a wavy snake, a sketchy lumpy human, a few dotty bits of bookkeeping. Not big, not flashy, but unmistakable, a lighter red against the flat red of the surrounding plane. An idea, executed: spiral, snake, man, and man's arithmetic. Without warning there were petroglyphs everywhere, and the wealth of them was exhausting and humiliating. We'd obviously been driving by them for a long time and had simply failed to notice. "There," I said. "There. And over there." I pointed almost listlessly, in disbelief. How could we not have *seen*?

Many of these petroglyphs are estimated to be 1,200 years old, but it is not age that makes them interesting. They speak in sine waves, orbs, blots, and wiggles; people have three legs, feet shaped like hairpins, heads like television sets, and fat arms coming from their ears. They sit on the rock and defeat the viewer with their inarticulate urgency; the message is packed with meaning, but the meaning also keeps escaping—here are things we can call beasts and men, over here are more things we can call lines and circles, but there is something inadequate in this naming. They are both old and utterly new, especially to the blinking and startled soul who has never seen them before. The petroglyphs are about something, but much of their raw, detailed, unmetaphoric beauty is in their resistance. They don't care about us, and they don't accommodate. They point wildly and repeatedly at something it is no longer possible to see. The jolt is unmistakable.

I have to add that some of the images in Nine Mile Canyon have been ruined by mindless and perhaps drunken latecomers. We are particularly displeased with George W., 1912, who felt the need to announce his existence at the expense of a Fremont ideogram. There is a cave, shallow and broad but good shelter from the weather, where some grouchy soul has painted a warning: PRIVATE PROPERTY. NO TRESPASSING. The letters run across a mural of the plump running creatures of the valleys, fuguing sideways and upward toward some ancient destination. In the same cave, a large semicircle of rock has been cold chiseled away—somebody liked the petroglyph enough to steal it. It is a maddening thing to see, intrusive and stupid, and yet some corner of me understands. Once you see these petroglyphs, you do want to make one of your own. Not to deface, not even to copy, but to see what's really involved, to find out how hard it is to do, and to test the intention of the original artist.

Because it is art, there is no mistaking that. And it's everywhere, on every likely-looking bit of flat billboard space in an abundance that is unhinged and merry and individual. In this terribly dry place where rocks slip and ankles turn over, where the blunt needles of the canyon walls are hopelessly high, is this celebration of images, images everywhere. Pictures picked out in small dots into the soft sandstone, pictures painted with substances best not imagined, pictures hung with the abandon of a preschool.

Confronted with all this, I had a wonderful failure of the imagination. It seemed to me that something in me had to change to accommodate this thrust of energy, this ancient and puzzling display. It was untamed and troubling and enchanting, and it forced me to revise my ideas about things and people. There in that canyon, for the first time in my tense, vigilant, unobservant life, I saw how little time I have and how little space I occupy.

COMPARED TO THE EPIPHANIES of Thoreau this looks pretty trivial, but it was my epiphany, and it stuck with me in that tiresome way epiphanies do. Without preamble, the familiar cultural landscape of my home state suddenly seemed full of complex and urgent little mysteries; things I had been gliding over now seemed to hold the promise of moral and aesthetic traction. Vermont seemed different, less familiar, and more compelling. Where else but here is here? How could we ever replace it?

Our physical and cultural geographies have an embedded genius that I think and hope will transcend the flattening that comes with the noisy arrival of chain stores and cellular telephones. In a more predictable introduction, this would be the part where I scold developers and rant about the absorption of the American countryside into *generica*, a new word for a new place that looks like every other place. It is generica that plagues the outskirts of every medium-sized city with its strip malls and fast-food stops and traffic lights; it is generica that always persuades me to drive off quite confidently in the wrong direction. I'm not going to rant: I secretly enjoy the drippy food and the discount electronics and feel a kind of stunned wonder at the sheer abundance and muddle of American commercial enterprise. These, too, are a kind of petroglyph, a perverse writing in stone that tells a perverse story, so I will leave the yelling about how bad it is to people who really enjoy raising their voices.

Instead, I offer up this travel-antitravel book. These essays may persuade you to make an inexpensive but satisfying junket to Vermont, or they may persuade you there is no wonder greater than the one of being exactly, precisely where you are. Or, if I have been a really good magician, both. Either way—whether you travel or antitravel—I hope the wonder and the complexity of this world of ours shines through.

As a practical matter, this book does not cover what I think of as the Big Stuff—the radiant but rather pricey experience of spending the day at the Shelburne Museum or walking the upscale brick sidewalks of Woodstock, Manchester, or Stowe. I understand that these are real pleasures, but they are not my kind of pleasure—checkbook tourism makes me tired. I can sometimes even work myself into a gentle frenzy over all the travelers who come to Vermont, do only the Big Stuff, and carry away, triumphantly, a wooden duck decoy with a little plaid ribbon tied around its neck. The duck isn't bad, but it is inadequate: Vermont would be a sorry place if that were all the magic we could manage.

I have also made no effort to be general, thorough, or encyclopedic; for every place I visit here there are ten others, sleeping in the valleys or hiding in plain sight under the slanting sun. Nor is this an insider's guide to places off the beaten track, or at least I don't think it is—any book that includes the rest stops along the interstate can hardly make a claim like that. But there is an element of that in here, and I only hope it is without the implicit snobbiness that all those off-the-beaten-track travel books trade so heavily in. These places are not cool, exclusive, or difficult to get reservations for, but merely overlooked and undervalued, unparsed or misunderstood. Everything discussed here is either cheap or free; a few places are inconvenient but well worth the trouble. Two of the places—Aspet and the Bread and Puppet Museum—probably qualify as Big Stuff but are in here anyway because of the visual challenges and deep satisfactions they offer certain visitors.

Because life is cumulative, and because this is the way my mind works, I've clustered like things with like, even though they may be separated by many miles. Thus you probably can't enjoy the dizzy pleasure of the Dowser's Labyrinth, the Round Church, and Captain Thunderbolt's schoolhouse in a single day, but you can go to one and meditate on the others. I've left out, regrettably, several exhilarating sites because they are on private property, are delicate places that can't withstand much traffic, or are destinations that are primarily commercial establishments. This last does not point to a disapproval of commerce so much as a disapproval of shopping as a form of entertainment. In truth, nothing would give me greater pleasure than directing all visitors of all nations to Junior Sanderson's hardware store in Felchville, where it seems everything happens in good time for the right reasons, but, unless you really want hardware, you are going to get underfoot. Junior has work to do.

A book like this is never finished. I say this selfishly, to deflect criticism for things I have missed or excluded, and I say it truthfully, because, well, it is true. As I write this I mourn the passing of a wax museum in Manchester Center that closed its doors before I could get there to see it—I've always wondered what a wax museum in its final decline would be like, and whether the effigies on display would have little wicks coming out of their heads. I recently drove through Athens (pronounced Ay-thens) to the village of Cambridgeport and admired the four-story ruins of a mill. Like a lot of mills it periodically set itself on fire, and at some point in the late 1870s the owners got tired of rebuilding it. In 1978 *Yankee* magazine announced that the entire town was up for sale, which may be a cautionary tale about mills and the fragility of local economies, but turned out on inspection to be overstatement. No matter—I got to spend an afternoon among tumbled masonry, which makes me happy, and to talk with the owner of the general store about the hotel and its ballroom, now long gone, that had springs in the floor.

My point is the richness of life and the treasures in it, and how we lose these things in a world that seems to be mostly about speed and cash. The long, watchful pause is better than the high admission; the silent and enduring witness of a single stone can easily trump a thousand wooden duck decoys, provided it is the right stone. And there are a lot of stones in this book—markers, caves, sculptures, and headstones—mostly because stone is the chosen material for our important and enduring messages. At first I wondered if all the stones were here by accident, filling the book the way leftovers accumulate in the refrigerator, but now I don't think so. It could be, instead, that stone is the opposite of speed and money, being so ubiquitous and so still.

THAT SAID, there is the problem of subversiveness. It's a scary word, evoking people in dark clothes carrying concealed weapons, but this is not the evocation that I want or mean. What I mean to imply is that there is an underground, rather private quality to this book, a willingness to turn toward the unknown, to take chances, to shed ideas, and to accept discomfort in exchange for something else.

This, finally, is all I am proposing. Too often we do not travel to go and see, but to go richly and quickly and inflict our idiotic problems on strangers. This kind of travel goes in search of sameness; it encourages generica, which is something we already have in abundance. Worse, it encourages tourism's themes and packages and its reduction of our adventures to digestible little tropes, like pills. Travel becomes a new kind of medication.

If we are game for something new, then there is only one thing left to do. We must go and see and give the world our undivided attention. If we go the easy way and look around generically, we will see exactly what we expect to see: generica. Which may be reassuring, but it's also boring and blurry. The radiance of life is not worth much—and is not even much in evidence—if it does not fall on something and tease out both loveliness and a few worrisome, authentic shadows.

I hope you will come to Vermont and carry this book here with you; I hope the cover creases and fades and gets one of those sticky round stains that is the final watermark of adventure. But I also hope, with a subversive pleasure in defeating my own purpose, that you will outmaneuver this invitation and go a few miles down your own roads in your own place, parsing the landscape and reading the rocks of home.

Taken for Granite

An Afternoon in Hope Cemetery

I'VE BEEN TOLD AT LEAST TWICE THAT HOPE CEMETERY in Barre is the most beautiful cemetery in the country. This smacks of overstatement, but it's an overstatement worth exploring—it is true that the unusual headstones undulate over the hill almost surrealistically, like heraldic beasts cresting a wave as they swim toward some impossible destination. It is also true that the gates are elegant and parabolic and border on the heroic; the durable Barre granite looks washed and new. And, despite the grand entrance, there is an informal quality to the headstones in Hope Cemetery, a whimsicality you don't normally associate with burial. A half-scale racing car, complete with safety netting on the windows, marks the final resting place of Joey LaQuerre, who drove at the local track and died in a snowmobiling accident when he was twenty-six. "Speed was his life," is his wife's comment. Nearby is a granite soccer ball and the coach's inscription: THERE IS NO ROOM FOR SECOND PLACE. THERE IS ONLY ONE PLACE, AND THAT IS FIRST PLACE. Not far away a biplane mounts through the clouds, fully rendered in three dimensions, and over here, Mr. Bettini's stone easy chair invites you to sit. On a gloomier note, Louis Brusa droops in his wife's arms, forever dying of the stonecutter's disease, silicosis.

It is beautiful in a quirky, defiant way, and the stones tug at your sleeve and drag you from place to place. Here is the huge capital A for Arnholm; there is the Fontana marker with its oak, its arches, and its portraits; and over there is the Catto monument, a smooth and energetic abstraction pointing at the sky. It looks like it will board in three minutes—have your tickets ready, please. There is no soft marble here, only granite, and when the sun hits the monuments you can almost hear a high note, a sort of melody in local stone.

The only trouble with cemeteries is that the people in them are all dead. It could be that the stones seem animate because the people aren't. You feel this with the dead children, of which there are always too many, and the people slain by tuberculosis and influenza. You feel this with all the women named Mother, and all the men dead before their prime. In particular, you feel this at the grave site of Elia Corti, who looks forever southward with his mustache drooping, the tools of his trade chiseled at his feet.

Called Eli and, like many of Barre's Italians, a stonecutter, he was shot on Saturday, October 3, 1903, at Socialist Hall. That evening an uproar took place between socialists and anarchists who had converged to hear a speaker, a fellow from New York named Serrati. Serrati was a socialist and newspaper editor who had said unkind things about anarchists, particularly the Barre anarchists: He referred to them, in his *Il Proletario*, as "counterfeiters," "liars," and "ruffians." This was strong language, and perhaps language that encouraged him to dawdle as he approached the town. In any case, he was late, and the crowd waited with decreasing patience; soon the jostling began. Words were exchanged. Alex Garetto, who later claimed self-defense, pulled out a pistol and fired twice into the crowd; Corti was hit at close range and died around midnight the following day.

IT SOUNDS ALMOST QUAINT from our comfortable perch at the end of the twentieth century. Anarchists, socialists, explosions—it all seems terribly grainy somehow, wild but far away. Our smugness lets us forget about the strikes, the labor movement, and the political changes that polarized the country, and our memories don't include the five-month work stoppage in 1902 by the United Mine Workers that effectively crippled the economy, pushing the price of coal from five dollars a ton to fourteen dollars. But that is what happened. There were threats, assassinations, and uprisings; to the social fathers and the captains of industry, it must have seemed that men with accents and peculiar surnames were everywhere elbowing their way to the front of the crowd, where they shouted demands.

And Barre was in the thick of it. Radical visitors to this rural hotbed of activism included Emma Goldman, Eugene Debs, Big Bill Hayward, and Samuel Gompers. During the strikes in the textile mills in Lawrence, Massachusetts, the people of Barre opened their homes to the strikers' children in a show of solidarity. The appearance of speakers like Serrati was a fairly common occurrence, though for the most part these events did not end quite so badly.

The *Barre Daily Times* of October 5, the Monday following the shooting, attributed the Corti incident to a long-standing feud between the anarchists and the socialists; Garetto was a socialist while most of the crowd was of the anarchist persuasion. After Corti was hit, said the *Daily Times*, "every anarchist in the hall jumped at Garetto and he was unceremoniously knocked downstairs, striking his head and getting several bad cuts and bruises. When Garetto reached the bottom stair he got on his feet as quickly as possible and ran—ran for his life up Granite Street, through West Street, up Summer Street, through Elm Street, across the square, into the city building, and into Judge Fay's office." There he crouched in a corner and pleaded with Judge Fay to protect him. In this way we are reminded of an important difference between socialism and anarchy: Socialists have great and perhaps undue faith in government.

THREE YEARS BEFORE this unplanned explosion of partisan violence, Eli Corti had been peacefully chipping away on the bas-relief panels at the base of the Robert Burns monument that graces the sloping lawn in front of the old Spaulding High School. And he was doing a swell job: This particular statue is a testament to how hard stone, in the right hands, can become fluid and animate; it is also a testament to the oblique resonances of American history. Here in central Vermont, an Italian stonecutter was making his artistic reputation for his work on a statue of a Scottish poet who had died a hundred years before. How's that for long-distance and multicultural? And, of course, tragic: Burns had died young, but he still managed to outlive Corti by three years.

If you visit the statue today and look at Corti's work, it's hard not to think about the keening, pervasive homesickness Burns sometimes invoked and was probably felt by this native of Viggiù. His heart was not in the highlands, but he carved the Burns cottage in Ayrshire with complex affection, wheelbarrow and all. It was a home, and it was far away, and this was a constellation generally understood in turn-of-the-century Barre.

Barre teemed with immigrants, attracted by the granite trade. In 1880 the population was about two thousand, and by 1900 the head count was climbing toward twelve thousand. The first wave was mostly Scots and the second mostly Italian, but in the mix were Norwegians, Swedes,

Spaniards, Irish, Greeks, and French Canadians. It was a rough-edged town with a certain gritty pride—even the way it was named is placed in the context of a brawl. The story, certainly apocryphal, is that two men from Massachusetts wrestled for the honor of naming the place after their respective hometowns. After mixing it up, Jonathan Sherman from Barre pinned Joseph Thompson from Holden: "There, by God," he proclaimed, "the name is Barre." The truth—that the name was selected by Ezekial Wheeler, who had ponied up the largest gift toward building a church—lacked noise and color.

Eli Corti had been in America about twelve years before getting caught up in the crossfire of history. Oddly enough, he does not appear to have been either a fervent anarchist or a fervent socialist—contemporary accounts seem almost insistent on this point, although he was probably allied with somebody in some way or another. The day he died he had attended a funeral and eaten supper with friends on Granite Street, and he showed up at the speaker's hall mostly because others did, following the social logic of almost any public gathering. After the shooting, the hall emptied in a flash—Corti was taken across Granite Street to wait for a doctor while everybody else hotfooted it back home. By the time the police arrived the hall was utterly, almost eerily empty. The speaker, Serrati, who had turned up after the shooting, was found in the co-operative store that was housed in the same building. He seemed confused but was perhaps merely inarticulate since he didn't speak any English. Through an interpreter, he had the following exchange with a *Daily Times* reporter:

"Where were you at the time of the shooting?"

"I think I was on Railroad Street at the time, being about to start for the Socialist Hall."

"Did anyone attempt to interfere with you or harm you in any way on your way to the hall?"

"No, but at about six o'clock a man slapped my face."

This slapping business seems to have been of a piece with Serrati's talk about ruffians and counterfeiters; "Not knowing who or what to blame," the officers took Serrati into custody. They also didn't know that the man they really wanted was back at the now-empty police station, nursing his wounds from his ejection down the stairs. Judge Fay had sent him there and told him to wait, and he had waited, and passed the next several days waiting some more, rolled up in a blanket in a holding cell, immobilized by guilt, worry, and grief.

The same guilt and grief rolled through the community and is audible in newspaper accounts and obituaries. Corti, "one of the most peaceable of citizens," became a moral lesson about fractiousness and how it backfires. He was innocent, talented, and ultimately harmless, to say nothing of levelheaded: "I am shot," Corti told his fellow citizens. "Run for a doctor."

The wound, the *Daily Times* pointed out, was very similar to the one that had killed President McKinley at the Pan-American Exposition in 1901. Which, despite its surface acceptability, still seems like a very unusual thing to say. It is true both men were shot in the abdomen, although McKinley was a politician who died of gangrene and Corti was a stonecutter who died of shock and damage to his spinal cord. What really links the two shootings is the idea of a marginal and intemperate person waving a gun: Leon Czolgosz or Alexander Garetto—what's the difference? And it was after the McKinley assassination that the United States began testing its immigrants for political soundness—a test, we are subtly led to believe, Eli Corti would have passed. Or not. Either way he is elevated, perhaps martyred, and his death climbs another rung of meaning.

In one man it seems that many things fold together, and the outpouring of sorrow over Corti's death culminated in the grave marker in Hope Cemetery. Here, a slender and rather ordinary fellow rests his head on his hand and looks vaguely heroic but vaguely puzzled—he seems to wonder, as I do, what really happened. At his feet are his tools: calipers, hammer, chisel, square, and the then-newfangled pneumatic carving tool. Grieving stonecutters from across Vermont contributed this final touch, and the recursiveness of stonecutting tools carved in stone by stonecutters in a stonecutter's memory is a melancholy, complicated pleasure that is hard to beat.

I GREW UP misunderstanding things. As a child of the Cold War, I always pledged "a legion" to the flag, and thought the road sign, THICKLY SETTLED, meant the village we downshifted through had reached a very high degree of consensus. I also took things "for granite"—things that were hard, reliable, and beyond dispute—and took them seriously. Standing in the hot sun in front of this elaborate gray marker, I feel a shimmering, not altogether pleasing doubleness. I realize that these stonecutters, too, were taken for granite: crushed in the quarries or coughing up the bloody gray mess that signaled silicosis. Or, like Corti, taken by an accident of granite's history—a delayed speaker, an anarchist tool sharpener, a Scots poet, an expansionist president, and a loose bullet. He lived, according to the paper, long enough to direct his own funeral. Keep it simple, he said: "No band."

I like this final assertion in the same way I like Corti's humble little wheelbarrow outside a poet's house in a country far away, and it's a very American liking. Hope Cemetery closes the loop between life and death, but not tightly; everywhere around the graveyard is evidence of the insistent, percolating, doomed individual. It's a blue-collar town with a high-end burial ground, wedged on marginal farmland between what used to be the poor farm and the dump. It is because of these things, and not despite them, that I decide the overstatement is true: This probably *is* the most beautiful cemetery in America.

To get there: Take I-89 to exit 7, and follow the signs for Route 62 and Barre. The divided highway ends at Main Street with a set of lights. Go straight through these lights past the Italian American Monument, and follow Maple Avenue up the hill. The Merchant Street Extension will come in on your right, and Hope Cemetery, with its curved gates, will soon appear on your left.

Cars are allowed, and the cemetery is big enough to make bringing a car tempting. It is the final home of six thousand people and—trust me—the variety and exuberance of the carving is touched on only briefly here. No formal tours are offered, but there is a self-tour pamphlet available from the city of Barre. Call 802-476-6245.

Justin Morgan Had a Life

A Man and His Horse

U P A BACK ROAD IN TUNBRIDGE, MAYBE A MILE OR so beyond the Flint Bridge, is the gravestone for Justin Morgan. It's a newish stone—it doesn't tilt and there's no moss—and if you read it at all carefully you learn it isn't really a gravestone at all. Gravestones say HERE LIES. This says, with a vague and cheerful gesture, ON THIS FARM. Justin Morgan isn't here, exactly, but he's somewhere around here. This may be what happens sometimes when you put up a marker for a horse.

The other Justin Morgan, the human one, is buried in the Randolph Center cemetery; if you go there you may find the stones, notes, and flowers I found. "Thank you," said one message, "for my horse. Thank you." It's hard not to wonder if Mr. Morgan would find this note confusing should he wake up and read it, having missed all the events of the intervening years. His horse outlived him by more than two decades and was probably known to him simply as Figure, a small, rough-coated, perky yearling he had acquired in Springfield, Massachusetts, as partial payment of a debt.

If you don't like horses much, your attention is probably wandering about now. I hope you will stay with me here because this is not a story about girls and their ponies, but about how American myths are made. This little bay with the curving crest and short back singlehandedly transformed our ideas about equine usefulness—Morgans, unlike other breeds, really are all things to all people. They are quick, comfortable, front-loaded, alert, and packed with attitude—your correspondent, who grew up around Thoroughbreds, warmbloods, and Quarter Horses, lost her hard little heart to a Morgan in her middle age. Nowhere is there a breed that so characteristically wants to know what we are doing and what comes next—Thoroughbreds condescend, Quarter Horses take notes, but a Morgan volunteers. They meet you at the gate and ask importunate questions: Are we going to the fire tower? Will we school in the ring? Any chance of giving some kid a pony ride?

A fifteen-hand Morgan could pull stumps all morning, win a trotting race after lunch, and drive the family into town in the evening; Morgans today compete in endurance rides, teach disabled students basic horsemanship, cut cattle, go over fences, and win coaching competitions. They could probably juggle and play piano if they only had more fingers; if there is any breed you are going to allow into the house, it's going to be a Morgan. All this and comfortable, too—their well oiled gaits derive directly from their wide backs and their foursquare architecture.

Figure—or Justin Morgan as he came to be known—was the only American horse to initiate, with one set of genes, an entire breed. He was so prepotent that any old mare would do. All his offspring rose from the ground, shook themselves, and began asking questions: Who are you? How about a game? Can we go to the parade? And they all looked the same, with their wide chests and small ears and round, hard feet. Their necks arch, their nostrils are nearly prehensile, and their bones appear to be made of Barre granite. They adore the mud, and adore having the mud removed—they lean into the dandy brush with audible groans of pleasure and are as pleased as you are with the dark silk that emerges and catches the sun. I look pretty good, they say. Now what?

THAT SAID, it must also be said that Justin Morgan the man has become utterly submerged in his ownership of a horse, and even the most perfunctory review of the facts proves this isn't fair. Morgan came with his family to Randolph in 1788, took up teaching and music, and was almost immediately elected to the positions of lister and grand juryman. He went on to serve as town clerk, an exalted station even (or perhaps especially) in the current century. Town clerks know a little bit about everything and quite a lot about everyone—the position requires discretion, patience, and an even hand, things Morgan apparently had. In West Springfield, Massachusetts, he had managed a breeding stable and, at least briefly, sold spirits on a retail basis out of his home.

This subverts a common popular myth of Morgan as a frail, lonely schoolmaster who acquired Figure by pure accident. He may have been frail by farming standards— he couldn't perform heavy farm labor—but he was not the reticent, rather limp personality that appears in popular fiction. Granted, at least two of these novels were written for young readers: In *Justin Morgan Had a Horse*, by Marguerite Henry, Morgan the man is decidedly mousy, and is deprived of his wife and family and upstaged by a boy. In *Justin Morgan, Founder of His Race*, by Eleanor Waring Burnham, Morgan is allowed to keep the large family he really had, but it is a young girl from away who recognizes Figure's true potential. This popular image is exactly that—a popular image. When we weave our myths, we change reality: if we cannot make Morgan larger than life, it suits us to make him smaller.

Morgan the man was a competent composer; one of his pieces, called "Montgomery," has been described by the musicologist Alan Buechner as "[o]ne of the hundred psalm and hymn tunes most frequently printed in American tune books of the eighteenth century. . . . It is the only tune by a Vermonter to be so distinguished." As late as 1966, his music was still in print in the *Original Sacred Harp*, published out of Atlanta. Other notable compositions were "Amanda" and the "Judgment Anthem." He raised five children in Randolph Center, and one of them, Justin Jr., went on to represent the town of Stockbridge in the House of Representatives and to serve as the senator from Windsor County.

Morgan knew good horses. From his Massachusetts breeding barn he advertised the stud services of Beautiful Bay, who is possibly Figure's sire, and Diamond, the possible sire of Figure's dam. True, the colt had surprises in store, but horses are full of surprises—I once knew a horse that would eat a ham sandwich and another that would only ride backward in the trailer, where she ogled cars over the tailgate. You get used to these things. What I can't get used to is the idea that Morgan was a wimp, and I argue that Justin Morgan had a life; the record shows that he was an educated man with a gift for writing fugues and melodies, a public servant, a good father, and, when it came to horses, one smart cookie. His sin in the eyes of twentieth-century writers was his basic modesty and his allergy to self-promotion.

In 1795 Morgan advertised in the *Rutland Herald:* "Figure will cover this season at the stable of Samuel Allen in Williston, and at the stable in Hinesburgh, formally owned by Mr. Munson. Figure sprang from a curious horse owned by Col. DeLancey of New York, but the greatest recommendation I can give him is that he is exceedingly sure, and gets curious colts."

This ad was written when Figure was three or perhaps nearing four, a time when his remarkable traits were becoming obvious. Yet the announcement is restrained—other horses offered for stud in the same newspaper seem to trace their excitable lineage directly to Pegasus. Extravagant claims were commonplace; Figure, on the other hand, is merely "curious." Which he certainly was—there is not a Morgan alive who does not wish to know the contents of your pockets—but in the eighteenth century this word often pointed to refinement, intelligence, and dexterity.

The same use of curious could be applied just as easily to Morgan himself. Though he was never a financial success, he wrote his music, taught his pupils, served the town, did a little light farming, and died in possession of a small, useful library and a saddle and bridle. But, sadly, no horse—Figure had been traded on, and would be bought and sold many times in his twenty-nine years. Morgan the man was buried where he lived, in Randolph Center, where his dark-slate gravestone has been replaced with modern granite: THIS MAN BROUGHT TO VERMONT THE COLT FROM WHICH ALL MORGAN HORSES ARE DESCENDED, it says. And, in the lower left corner, like a footnote, the inscription, PERPETUAL CARE. The original headstone is in the possession of the Randolph Historical Society and announces that he died at fifty-one. It says nothing at all about Figure. It was carved in 1798. Who knew?

IF MORGAN THE MAN has been submerged by Morgan the horse, then at least it has been done in a worthy cause. And a local one—the story of the Morgan horse seems to circle back persistently to Randolph, as if there is something in her high farms and cold winters that meshes with the temperament of the breed. As Morgans carried their owners west to the prairies and south to the Civil War, the distinctive body, tiny ears, and remarkable disposition got diluted; as the automobile encroached and began honking its horn, the breed was nearing extinction. Then in 1927 Robert Lippitt Knight, who owned the Green Mountain Stock Farm in Randolph, acted on a tip from his feed delivery man and purchased the breeding stock of Vermont horseman A. Fullerton Phillips. Phillips had dedicated his time, his money, and some say his life to preserving the Morgan line, but in 1922, a part of Phillips's herd was out to grass and was struck by lightning. Twelve of the thirteen horses died instantly, and the last one lost her composure and had to be destroyed later on. The only surviving horses were the ones who happened to be in the barn; it is said that Phillips died of a broken heart a few years later. When the estate and the horses came up for sale, Knight brought two stallions and four mares to the Stock Farm, and the rebirth of the Morgan in what is now called the Lippitt line was begun.

From these Randolph beginnings, the Morgan breed has become part of the American landscape—Morgan genes have improved the Saddlebred, the Quarter Horse, the Hackney, the Tennessee Walking Horse, and the Standardbred. And the Morgan attitude has improved we humans, allowing us to borrow their alertness, smarts, determination, and tractability.

WHEN WE BORROW, we also have an obligation to repay, and in this case the debt is owed to Mr. Morgan. The story goes that Morgan, frail and dithering, dragged this colt sadly up the Connecticut River Valley to Vermont, trying to sell him along the way. Which he undoubtedly was—all horses, to a breeder, are always up for sale. But the implication is that he was trying to offload Figure out of ignorance, and there is no evidence that Morgan was an ignorant man. He almost certainly knew what all good horsemen know: Diminutive, funny-looking horses often hold up their end of the bargain in the field. The only thing he didn't know, and couldn't, was that this odd-looking creature was a genetic sport that carried in his genes enough dominant information to last many generations.

The problem of Figure's breeding has triggered further mythmaking, and one account traces Figure's bloodlines to the stallion True Briton, a celebrated pacer who won several important match races before the Revolution. Another account traces him back to Wildair, the same stallion that produced the line that led to the Thoroughbred sire Nasrullah. Both claims are fishy and seem to be grounded mainly in chronology: These other horses were alive and in New England at about the right time. There is an air of retrofit to these explanations, like a mail-order coat of arms, and the plain truth is that nobody knows with any certainty where Figure came from. Perhaps he sprang whole from the dark soil of a frontier valley, and if we must make myths, this one is more satisfying—Figure wears the flexible, intelligent expression of a commoner.

Figure looks, at least to my eyes, much more like Justin Morgan than is generally imagined—the sickly, impoverished, and rather tedious man who haunts the literature is as much a construction as these imagined noble bloodlines. Yet the myth is useful, because it points to a mystery: How does this kind of excellence happen by sheer accident? The beauty of the horse seems to require some kind of storytelling, and I only argue that the tale is just as good when Morgan the man suffers no collateral damage. He served as well as most and better than many, and died too soon to hear the end of his own story.

Because of these myths, and because of the truth that is accidentally captured in them, it is worth a pilgrimage to Randolph Center to say hello to a dead musician and schoolteacher, and another visit to Tunbridge to visit Figure, even though Figure isn't buried exactly there. Both places say different things about our history, and Figure's marker has a grassy lawn, a little fence, and a tended look that is satisfying without being excessively mournful or reverent. ON THIS FARM, it reads, and the vagueness seems appropriate somehow. Figure is on this farm and on many others, chinning the gate, shedding his halter, exploring the swamp, and plying his owners with his endless questions.

To get there: Find Figure's marker by traveling on Route 110 through Tunbridge and turning at the Flint covered bridge. A small green marker signals the turn, but after this the signage gets a little skimpy. After the bridge go right, and climb to Harolyn Hill Road; go right onto Harolyn Hill, and pull over pretty much right away. Figure's marker is nearest the turn, and another horse is buried nearby. There is a story in this second marker, but I don't know what it is.

The grave of Justin Morgan the man is in the cemetery next to the Randolph Center School House and across from the south campus of Vermont Technical College. From I-89, take the Randolph exit, go east and up the hill, and then turn right at the top where you see the main campus gate directly in front of you. Continue a short way, until you see a white church on your left; turn left and park, if it's summertime, in the schoolhouse lot. The grave is about two-thirds of the way toward the back of the cemetery, where the older stones tend to be clustered, and about a quarter of the way in from the schoolhouse side of the cemetery. Other Morgan family members—his brother Caleb and his wife Martha— are buried nearby.

If you want to see a living horse, your best bet is the UVM Morgan Horse Farm outside of Middlebury in Weybridge. There they will try to persuade you that Colonel Joseph Battell saved the Morgans from extinction, and they are certainly welcome to their opinion. There are lots of Morgans ready to mug for a camera in and around Randolph, but they are privately owned; the remaining Morgans on the Stock Farm, which is now an inn, are not part of an active breeding program.

Facing West
The Joseph Smith Memorial

T HE MORMON PROPHET JOSEPH SMITH WAS BORN ON a hill farm in the Vermont piedmont. This piedmont, on the eastern slope of the Green Mountains, has a rumpled look, like a bath mat after three teenagers in succession have used the shower: Deep valleys alternate with open summits and shallow rivers. It's a part of the state that a friend of mine describes as "almost Irish"—haunted, green, rolling, full of folded-in surprises and queer little swamps at the tops of hills, as if water does not run downhill there, or if it does it merely saunters.

It's a good place for a prophet to be born. The Joseph Smith Memorial, tucked up on a back road off route 14 in Sharon, is one of those groomed places, marked by stonework and flower beds and (it's a little startling at first) hymns coming out of the shrubbery near the rest rooms. In summer the place smells of cut grass and bark mulch and masonry roasting peacefully in the sun. It hardly matters that the house where Smith was born doesn't amount to much anymore. It offers the eye a few cellarhole rocks in rough formation and one flat, heavy stone, more or less the same stone used as a threshold in houses everywhere across New England. But soaring into the sky next to this modest arrangement is a granite obelisk, and in the lap of this marker is a visitors' center. Behind all this, in the woods, are the remains of other houses, an old turnpike, a stone bridge over a brook, and other evidence of lost rural civilization. The Joseph Smith birthplace is also staffed by Mormons on mission, happy to see you and eager to help. Do you have questions? Would you like a tour? Do you know the prophet's story?

For a writer, and a rather lazy one at that, these happy guides appear to be a dream come true, because I do have a question. How is it, I ask them, that both Joseph Smith and Brigham Young, two heavy hitters in the Church of Jesus Christ of Latter-day Saints, came to be born in Vermont? In response, a courteous and eager researcher produces a list of no fewer than a dozen Vermont natives important to the Mormon story, complete with the dates, towns, and counties of birth. The list includes Oliver Cowdery, witness and one of the transcribers of *The Book of Mormon*; the apostles Heber Kimball, Erastus Snow, Albert Carrington, and Lyman and Luke Johnson; and church historian George Robinson. Other lights are Newel K. Whitney and Smith family members Hyrum and William.

"Sheesh," I say. "Look at them all."

As a bonus and a study aid, I am also offered a time line—"From Tunbridge to Palmyra"—that I realize later is not a standard handout but, like the list, was developed in response to my individual query. The Saints, as they are sometimes called, have a lively and doctrinally compelling interest in genealogy. I ask them again: Why are so many Vermonters important to the early Mormon church? Why here, when the church came into being west of here? And went on, farther west, into the unsettled unknown? It's an unfair question, and one I can see has very little resonance for them. The roots of Mormonism are here, they seem to be saying, because, well, um, that is where they are.

IT's A TOUCHY SUBJECT, Mormonism—the history of the movement is to some degree the history of them not getting along very well with their neighbors and being ejected and self-propelled across the massive American landscape. As a lapsed Quaker with tolerant inclinations, I am always secretly puzzled by the historical uproar surrounding the Latter-day Saints, and secretly impressed by their industry and their obsession with flowers. In Temple Square in Salt Lake City these flowers—tulips, petunias, kitten-faced pansies—can be seen everywhere, planted in mathematical rows and tended by twirling sprinklers. Here in Vermont, seedling begonias march through the bark mulch in the dappled shade, and something in their placement and spacing announces solidarity with their Utah cousins.

Walking the recommended loop through the woods, I think about Joseph Smith and his claims on our attention—he was a man of angels and gold plates, lost civilizations and mysteries, miracles and revelations. Some people say he was a con man and a moneydigger who dabbled in sorcery, and that he was licentious, advancing polygamy because it was a nicer word for what he was already practicing. Fraudulent, glib, bossy, prevaricating, seductive—the well of unpleasant things that have been said about the first prophet is deep and, like a well, curiously dark and narrow. Still, none of his detractors denies he set something big in motion, that he propelled people through time and space, and that he insisted strenuously on a commitment to a new set of moral values.

These are young, sunny woods, peppered with signs that direct attention to more cellarholes. I'm in a docile, sunny mood so I go and look, noticing again the tentative sadness of all abandoned places. This one is no different. There is an astringent, distanced expression to these kinds of ruins, even though, as a practical matter, the early nineteenth century is accessible and relatively recent. Look at it this way: In 1830, the year *The Book of Mormon* was published, Peter Cooper built the *Tom Thumb*, the first American steam locomotive; Louis Daguerre was monkeying around with silver iodide and giving birth to photography; and, up in St. Johnsbury, Vermont, Thaddeus Fairbanks was devising the platform scale. But looking at these quiet ruins in the woods, with their lost, minimalist expressions, 1830 seems like a forever or two ago. I know this is a place where something important happened, but it is difficult to say exactly what.

Smith claimed that *The Book of Mormon* was transcribed from a set of gold plates he found in Palmyra, New York, and that the plates were written in an Egyptian script he translated with the aid of Urim and Thummim, a sacred instrument that may have been a pair of spectacles but perhaps not. An angel, Moroni, led him to this treasure; the plates told the story of pre-Columbian America from 2,200 BC to about 420 AD. As history, *The Book of Mormon* is a troubling document since it depicts an advanced, homogenous culture not verified by the archeological record. Which is really too bad: Smith's prehistoric America had coins, sails, horses, wheels, steel, and, if I was paying close attention, elephants. I've read that the book has much in common—probably too much in common—with a novel written by one Solomon Spaulding at about the same time, and with another text called *View of the Hebrews*, printed five years earlier in 1825.

None of this shocks or bothers me. Perhaps it should, but good swiping, as Jules Feiffer once pointed out, is an art in itself. This is simply what writers do. Compiling speculative histories of the New World and its inhabitants was alluring because there were no tiresome facts to be accounted for, and there was a legitimate contemporary interest in the origins of Native Americans. Natives presented both practical and theological problems to the people on the frontier and were a powerful invitation to storytelling. But, but, but—I can almost hear Smith's critics objecting, balling their hands into fists—this is sworn to be sacred, revealed, and *true*.

Truth is a miserable business. *Bleak House* is true, despite its obvious falsity, and lots of people think the *Warren Commission Report* is false, despite its surface appearance of probity. I won't comment on this second title, though, because I've never read it right through to the end; its primary sin is that it's boring. The truth about truth is that it is contingent and multiple—just like the clean, open woods that offer up trails leading in various directions, with more helpful little signs. One, I notice, says PATRIARCH.

I look at this sign for a long time, trying to remember if the map at the mouth of the trail said anything about a patriarch hidden in the woods—you would think such a thing would come up. And you can't say "patriarch" in this particular context without semantic consequences: I peer up the trail and watch it wind away among the trees; I decide that this is something I really have to see.

It's a steep trail, but a fussy and tended one—there are little staircases and benches for the weary and a lazy stream that burbles to my left. There are no militant rows of flowers, but the trail has the same tended look I associate with the visitors' center and with Temple Square, two thousand miles away. I climb. It's fairly steep, but perhaps it ought to be, considering there's a patriarch up there.

VERMONT IN THE EARLY NINETEENTH CENTURY was in some ways pretty abysmal—the farm harvest was a mix of wool, milk, forage, and rocks. Better land to the west lured many away, including the Smith family, who apparently—though perhaps coincidentally—gave up on the state right after the infamous "year without a summer." In 1815 Mount Tambora in the East Indies erupted and did what volcanoes sometimes do: disrupted the climate. Atmospheric upset brought four killing frosts to Vermont between June 6 and August 30, 1816, along with several demoralizing falls of snow. This, combined with the normal challenges of thin soil and distant markets, made a lot of Vermonters look westward, where the Erie Canal was now under construction. I can almost see them, with their noses running and their hands red with chill, loading the wagons.

The same hardscrabble frontier conditions also helped trigger what is now called the Second Great Awakening, an upsurge in religious questing that effectively bit through the thick rope of eastern Calvinism. The result was Baptists, Methodists, and evangelists happily and earnestly off the leash, sniffing new spiritual frontiers.

Today, this movement away from the Puritan ethic seems inevitable—we don't approve of Puritans anymore, any more than we really understand them. But that isn't the point. The point is that there was something in the air, something unmediated and open-ended: Religious life was being transformed by the pioneer experience into something changeable, exhilarating, and perhaps a bit naughty.

Because we live in a secular age, we have a tendency to misunderstand religious revivals. We think they happen in church, and many of us think that church is where religious behavior ought to stay. Public enthusiasm for faith is in poor taste and may be a sign of mental instability: Lapel-grabbing fanatics haunt our airports but not our public imaginations. But when we think these thoughts, we are manipulating the wrong metaphor. The 1830s were in some ways like the late 1960s and early 1970s, when the nation was awash in the moral and civil unrest associated with the civil rights movement and the Vietnam War. In both eras, moral questions were urgent and public: In the earlier one, a person's spiritual stance and relationship with God was central to a person's being, and the urge to push the boundaries of worship was linked to the push westward and the movement of the frontier.

THE MOVEMENT UPWARD, following the trail I assumed would be short and easy, has become steep, endless, difficult, and tantalizing. Because it winds, it is possible that the end is always in sight, and because it winds, it never is. To my irritation and growing amazement, the cute trail with benches has shed its improvements and become a personal challenge. I won't quit, but I am muttering: *This had better be good.* As I climb I picture a stone man in a stone chair, hand upraised, or perhaps an enclosure, like a cellar hole, with an interpretive tablet inside. Or, I decide, a boulder, left behind by the glaciers, with a bronze caption sunk in its flank. Or, my thirsty body decides, a pretty spring, a silver cup, a little table. Maybe there's an eager, happy Saint up there, offering tracts and lemonade, and a paved road and a bus that will take me back down the mountain. I wish I'd worn better shoes, but there is no turning back now. I'm ready, after this long, patriarchal climb, for anything.

Except, of course, for what I find. Cresting the summit, I discover that the river valley unrolls like a papyrus at my feet and that the furry mountains, looking for all the world like bears asleep in sunshine, rest heavily on the near horizon. Squares of farmland poke through lines of trees, and scattered ponds glint like metal; the sky is a melting blue, like certain kinds of cobalt glass. I recognize nothing. Where on earth am I? I know that familiar valleys can look very different from a high vantage point, but for a long moment I have an idea that I have crossed a boundary into some alternate, glittering version of the Vermont piedmont, into a kind of fairyland. There is a shine—individual leaves on far-off trees reflect individual squares of sunlight, and a burnished raven hangs over a glassy pond. If I look carefully I can pick out the bright needle of the Smith Memorial below, which perhaps shimmers miraculously, simultaneously, in both worlds.

The high gloss, and the radical newness of things that ought to be old, both startles and comforts me—this unexpected shift in point of view offers a possible answer to my bumbling query. From the Patriarch I can see, obliquely, the roots of a religion.

It takes a few minutes for my surprise to wear off and for the place to become merely attractive, and I poke around the clearing. There is an abandoned fire ring, used recently, and a mound of bark mulch with a mystifying stick in the center—I can't decide if it's a living but pitiful tree, a marker, or a prank. The sweet, rolling breeze combs the yellow grass, and I realize that I've abandoned my men in chairs, my bronze plaques, and my lemonade concessions. These ideas have slipped away silently, embarrassed by their own inadequacy.

AT THE BOTTOM, back at the visitors' center, I ask one of the Saints about the Patriarch. Is it on church land? Where did it get the name? What does it mean? He is a young man, Asian-American, with a cast on one arm and a helpful, slightly edgy manner. He says yes, that is church land; it's called the Patriarch because, well, that is what it is called. He thinks it may have been named by the Smith family, but he really isn't sure. "You went up there?" he asks.

"Yes. It's quite an experience, don't you think?"

He gives me another one of his sweet, nervous smiles.

"I expected something different," I say, "but I wasn't disappointed."

"We had a group from Salt Lake City, a hundred and twenty of them, go up there yesterday."

"What did they do there?"

"Well," he explains without explaining, "it's very beautiful. In an unusual way, we think. But steep, as you know, and a long way."

I know perfectly well we are at mild cross-purposes— he would probably like to convert me, not knowing I am immune, and I would like to test drive an idea on him about the role of Vermont in making Mormons, not knowing how to begin. Neither of us knows what to say, so we look at the polished column, 38½ feet tall. Each foot equals one year in the life of the prophet—Smith was killed by an angry mob in Illinois in 1844. As I look, it occurs to me that almost exactly a year ago (or perhaps a foot) I stood in Emigration Canyon, outside of Salt Lake City, and cast an imaginary thread eastward, to the sleepy green hills of Vermont. Now, in Vermont, I think of the blue, impossible distances of the Wasatch Front, the flat mirror of the Great Salt Lake punctuated by the hunched backs of her islands, the furzy sprawl of the city with its temple spires sleeping in the sun. The canyon also offered a patriarchal view, a burnished glimpse of some other world.

We part ways without further questions, but we are not quite done. The next day I call and by luck get him on the phone. After a few preliminaries I get down to business. "Which way," I ask him, "does the monument face?"

"I've watched the shadows on it. I think it faces south."

"Are you sure?"

"I'm pretty sure."

"I want it to face west," I tell him.

"I know," he says. "So do I."

To get there: From I-89, take exit 3, and follow the sign at the bottom of the ramp for Royalton and the Vermont Law School. Go right at the Sugar House onto Route 14, and stay on this road past the iron bridge and the intersection of Routes 14 and 110. About three miles on, turn left—there is a sign—onto Dairy Hill Road, and climb about two miles. The Joseph Smith Monument is on your right. The entire complex covers 360 acres and includes picnic facilities and a campground.

The trek from the visitors' center to the summit of the Patriarch is, as I have tried to indicate, rather long and steep. Bring water, and don't try it unless you are in reasonably good physical condition.

The memorial is open year-round during the daylight hours, and tours of the grounds are offered on a seasonal basis.

Urban Glaciation
The Donohue Sea Caves

ORTHERN CARTOGRAPHIC, A COMPANY THAT MAKES
and prints good maps of Vermont, makes and
prints a good map of Burlington. On it is the
above-and-beyond information cherished by the idly curious: green parks the size of pencil boxes, the winding dot-
ted lines of bike paths, the striped beach umbrella for legal
places to swim. And on this map, just north of the older
part of the city and on the west edge of the flood plain
called the Intervale, is a green spot and, in seven-point
type, a label for the DONAHUE SEA CAVES. Which is spelled
wrong—the only error I have found on an otherwise flaw-
less publication.

But if it's spelled wrong, there is a reason—there, surrounded by the city, is a curiously reticent and inaccessi-
ble destination. Thus the sea caves expedition, mounted by
me and an old friend, began with a searching drive through
the Intervale on the Route 127 beltway, going slowly

enough to make the pickup behind us impatient. The map
hinted that the caves, if they were big enough, might be
seen from the highway, so we dawdled and looked west,
scanning the bluffs for breaks and shadows while the truck
behind us slid back and forth in the rear-view mirror, weaving
the way you do when you don't want to step on a toddler in
the supermarket. We saw a marshy pond, a bit of stockade
fencing, and a lot of damaged trees—Burlington was still
recovering from a winter ice storm that had come in like a
giant, flattening every third maple and snapping even the
ladylike, flexible birches. It was a big mess. We squinted
and talked: If the caves were small enough, we decided,
and the mess were big enough, they might be hidden under
the wreckage. At this exact moment the pickup accelerated
noisily and passed, and the young woman at the wheel gave
us a withering look. We waved, and she waved back a little dismissively. Then, suddenly, we were back in the city,
navigating the narrow maze of Burlington's Old North End.

So much for sea caves. We were resourceful and would
find something else to do.

Two weeks later, though, we found ourselves inexplic-
ably looking for the caves from above, from the landscaped
safety of a parking lot tucked in behind some town houses
along City Bluff. I was reading aloud, in my best school-
marmish manner, from the entry we had found in the Chittenden County Historical Society's *Historic Guide to
Burlington Neighborhoods.*

" 'One of the most interesting geologic phenomena in the Winooski Valley Park District are these limestone caves located on a fifteen-acre tract across from Route 127 from the southern portion of the Ethan Allen Homestead,' " I announced. " 'Donated by David Donohue to the district, these caves were created by wave action in the Champlain Sea over ten thousand years ago.' "

"That's nice to know," said Vince, my unindicted co-conspirator, gazing down at the tangled forest and the glint of water at the bottom, "but frustrating. How do we *get* to them?"

"It says here the caves are also known as the Devil's Den."

"Sounds like a hideout in a Hardy Boys mystery."

"What's this about a Champlain Sea?" I wondered.

"There ought to be a trail," Vince grumbled, "and it ought to start *here*."

THERE IS A TRAIL, just north of the bus stop, and a carved wooden sign that points the way. Never mind that it took us twenty minutes to find it; this trail is wide and promising and, were it not for the damaged, fallen trees, it would have made a fine wheelchair ramp. We frolicked down it through patches of sunshine and clouds of black flies, through woods that smelled of ferns and iron and moss on rocks. The cliff rose on our left side while the marsh assembled itself to our right. At the bottom, to our surprise, was the stockade fence we had seen from the Intervale road but with little rectangles cut into it at different levels, a kind of duck blind. We peered through these openings cautiously but did not see anything unusual—the marshy pond, the riff of breeze against the water, the parade of rusty Subarus on their way south. Still, impressed by all these amenities, we began looking for caves, picking our way through tufts of grass and mud along the rough shoulder of the cliff, pausing to gaze at cracks and cleavages. The marsh, slippery and fragrant, sent up gasses, while the rocks offered maidenhair fern and wild columbine.

We did find some clefts and cracks, and a few of them were deep enough to swallow a hand. "This is all very well," I ventured, lifting my sneakers out of the ooze with a sucking sound, "but I wouldn't call them caves."

"This can't be right," my companion said. "Read that description again."

" 'In few places does nature reveal herself in so many and such diverse aspects as here at the Devil's Den,' " I read. " 'On the one hand is a sense of grandeur, a great cave which stretches back into darkness spanned by massive vaults and arches of weather beaten rock which ascend in unbroken curves and cast dark shadows and reflections in the water at their base.' "

"Water where?"

" 'At their base.' "

"Then they have to be north of here, where the pond

is wider. What else does it say?"

" 'The approach to the Devil's Den, although at certain times of the year a bit boggy and difficult, is not entirely without charm.' "

"This must be one of those certain times of year,"
Vince said. His pants were brown with swamp water almost
to his knees.

"But there is charm, I think. It's not entirely without
charm. The book is right."

"It's not entirely without insects, either," said Vince,
flapping his hands. "Didn't it say something about arches
and grandeur and stuff?"

" 'A great cave which stretches back into darkness
spanned by massive vaults.' "

A cloud of mosquitoes, sensing food, descended.
"We're going about this entirely the wrong way," Vince
said.

I CALLED THE WINOOSKI VALLEY PARK DISTRICT, which
manages about eight hundred acres of green space, wet-
lands, and historic sites in and around the city, including
the Intervale and the Ethan Allen Homestead. There I
talked to Kate, who confirmed that the only way to get to
the Donohue Sea Caves was in a boat. "You could wade to
them in August if it's been dry, but in May I'd recommend
a canoe."

"Is it okay to do that? Will the boat police come and

arrest me if I put a canoe in the water there?"

"No boat police," she said serenely. "Not here."

"Is it true the caves were formed by the sea? Was there really a sea in Vermont?"

"I think there was. I can't tell you much about it, though."

"Was that a zillion years ago, two zillion, what?"

"Probably during the glaciers, whenever that was. Not zillions. Thousands, I think. But look, hey, I just remembered. There was some UVM geology professor who did something or other about those caves, and he went there. He can tell you more than I can."

"Have you ever been there?"

"I've seen them from the beltway."

"Are they big?"

"Pretty big. But you whiz by too fast to really appreciate them."

"Don't you think there's a little too much whizzing nowadays?"

Kate laughed. "I do."

AND SO, the next warm weekend, we hauled a rented canoe through the snags and downed trees; in the clear intervals between the ice damage Vince carried the canoe on his head, a trick I'd never seen. "Nothing to it," he lied. "I can't see, but otherwise this isn't difficult." My teenaged son, Nick, and I watched him progress like a huge mutant parrot through the forest and listened to his hollow, faraway commentary on the conditions inside. "Hundreds of mosquitoes," he reported, "but they aren't biting. Now there are thousands of mosquitoes. The boat is full of them, but I'm perfectly fine."

"Maybe they just need a ride to the bottom," Nick speculated.

"Maybe the canoe looks more inviting. Vince is tough," I said.

"Maybe it's the wrong time of year for them to bite," Nick added.

"Can you two please shut up and tell me where I am?"

The duck blind with its perforated fence appeared; not far beyond that we found a place to put the boat in. Wet only to our calves, we pushed off; down the pond a heron rose like a pterodactyl and stroked through the sky, offended. Dragonflies and damselflies clustered, curious, and the soup of the pond stirred, smelling like warm yeast. Fish swirled away and the sheet of algae closed behind them; the water basked under a buttery sun and a red-winged blackbird wobbled on a tall stalk and informed us we were trespassing.

Paddling north, with the bluffs to our left and the roaring beltway to our right, we at last slid around a stone shoulder to behold the caves. There are two—a tall keyhole with a high chimney, or window, and a second, smaller cave with a low, brooding expression. We looked, and the caves looked back. Across the sunny water they were dark and unreflecting, interesting but scary. Paddling carefully through the shallows toward these mouths of rock felt a little dangerous, like approaching an elephant that is said to be tame.

"If it's full of condoms and graffiti, I will be some pissed," I said.

"I doubt it will be. Getting here is *work*."

"But the city is right here. The high school is across the street."

"Shhh. We're getting closer."

There is something about a big cave that demands hush, much the way a church does. We pulled up the canoe and picked our way through the stumps and branches at the entrance and then stood, like a line of ducklings, looking in. It soared upward about thirty feet, backward about fifty. It was about forty feet wide. There was water and dripping and vaulting—all as described and promised but somehow better.

The main cave was smooth and intricate, with the organic curves of a child's castle partially ruined by the sea. Its roof soared upward and dripped cold, metallic water; the place smelled of minerals and damp and the exhale of old rocks. Sunlight stumbled partway in, absorbed by the sinuous dark walls. And, twelve feet up from the floor of the main chamber was a window, and through it we could see a leaning tree, fingers of fern, and a rough oval of sky.

At the far-off back of the cave, on a fist-sized ledge, was a bird's nest, abandoned. The cold water, covering a bed of rich mud, had logs and an old white bait bucket floating in it. But no condoms; no graffiti. We sensed it was as much itself as the day it was finished—if it is finished,—back when the glaciers receded.

JAMES MICHENER, the novelist, exasperates me—he can't seem to write about anything without starting with plate tectonics. The land rises and falls, lava flows, and dinosaurs die, and still there is no dialogue; his humans are midstory afterthoughts building toy towns out of matchsticks. I roll my eyes and throttle the fat, cheap paperback: *I know! I know! Now tell the story already!* Geology is all very well, but it sometimes lacks tension, energy, plot.

Geology becomes a good story, or at least a better one, when you stand inside it. How, I have to wonder, did these caves come to be exactly here? What made them? Why aren't there caves all along here, carved from the rock of City Bluffs? If one cave, why not many? What's all this business about an ocean?

Charles Johnson, in his 1980 book *The Nature of Vermont*, tells how in 1849 fossilized bones were found during the excavation of a railbed in Charlotte, Vermont, which is on Lake Champlain and south of Burlington. "First thought to be a horse," he writes, "they were later determined to be of a small whale, an extinct species but closely related to some whales that live today in Arctic waters. Along with this skeleton were found shells of clams and oysters, the same kind that now live in a cold marine environment. These facts suggest that indeed the whale lived in a cold ocean. But what ocean, and how did the whale get there?"

Like most competent writers, Johnson raises only questions he knows how to answer, and he goes on to divulge that Lake Vermont, the postglacial and much larger forerunner of Lake Champlain, was at one time saline. This happened when the oceans rose as the ice melted, sending salt water seeping down the St. Lawrence Valley. According to Johnson, this happened at least twice; there was water, sometimes fresh and sometimes brackish, covering most of the western half of the state. Some species of Champlain fish descend from saltwater species, and there is marine gravel at the foot of Mount Philo.

This shortwinded narrative proves that Michener could learn pith at Johnson's knee, and it does seem to settle any worries about the prehistoric ocean. But my practical, rather flatfooted mind is restless after the dark smell of the place, its echoes, its relentless specificity. The caves face to the east, toward the mountains and away from the lake, so if the caves were formed, as the Chittenden County Historical Society says, by wave action on an ancient shore, we may have a logistical problem. The sea was over there, and the caves have their back turned to it. Worse, if Johnson's maps are right, the caves were also submerged, perhaps by fathoms, in this putative ocean. And, finally, what kind of haphazard soul could find a fossil whale and decide it was a horse?

I NEED AN EXPERT, and I follow Kate's advice and call the University of Vermont's geology department. I explain that I want to know more about the sea caves, and that someone at the Winooski Valley Park District said that a professor there had seen the caves, or understood them, or knew something or other about them. Calling up people in Vermont is almost always a radiant experience—civil servants are civil, salespeople answer your questions, and university departments take long, detailed messages. I once called the governor's office and the governor herself answered; even the registry of motor vehicles, staffed nationwide by an army of crabby women in half-moon glasses, is staffed here by ordinary people who almost never tell you that you have waited in the wrong line, even if you have.

David Bucke, professor of geology, returned my call. He explained that the caves were probably not limestone but dolomite and that the rock was perhaps 550 million years old. Dolomite is a sedimentary rock, built up from the crumbs of other rocks, and is evidence of an ancient sea. But not, he explains, the same ancient sea: "I haven't visited these caves, but they are almost certainly post-glacial. The rock is much older and was probably formed, originally, within twenty degrees of the equator."

I have to think about this for a moment. I'm not sure I like it. It smacks of Michener.

"That's a long way from here."

"It is, but things got moved around."

"But what is a cave, exactly? How do caves happen?"

"Water," he says, succinctly. Vermonters are fun; they cut to the chase.

Water is intrusive—it finds its way through even the most inhospitable substances and carves a channel. Once that process begins it is almost impossible to stop: A little damp, and a lot of time, and bingo—you have huge, commercial caves like the ones in West Virginia and Missouri and smaller caves, like this one. But he's talking, I realize, about water in the ground, not the action of waves on a shoreline. I have to wonder: Is it correct to call these sea caves, or is it not?

"These are smooth," I tell him, "like a sand castle. Aren't the other kinds of caves sort of pointy?"

"Some caves are pointy and some caves are smooth," Bucke explains. "It depends on the kind of rock and the speed of the water—fast water can make those curvy surfaces." But he's honest: He hasn't been to the Donohue Sea Caves and can't say for sure whether they are true sea caves or not. "That pond in the Intervale is part of Lake Champlain," he says. "It rises and falls when the lake does. They are connected, and I can certainly imagine a sort of estuary. What's harder to imagine is enough wave action to make the caves if they really are as big as you say."

Rod Pingree, a Bolton geologist with a deep affection for Vermont's caves, attributes the Donohue Caves to dissolution, not necessarily erosion. "The Winooski River has swung around quite a lot, and that marsh is probably an old oxbow. The vaulted ceiling is typical of what are called solution dome pits, and it was formed when the water was much higher. They are not true sea caves." He notes, as I have already, that they face in the wrong direction.

"Want to hear some stories about that cave?" he twinkles.

Of course I do.

"There's a persistent rumor that the back of the cave you saw is not the end of it—that it goes back much farther, through the bluff, as far as the Burlington High School. There was an old quarry on the high-school site, and you hear about a cave opening there; they sealed it up when the school was built."

"For safety reasons," I say.

"For lots of reasons. But here's something else. I was in a restaurant, and I overheard a conversation about the cave. The person talking was a member of the family that once owned them, and he said he remembered the cave going much deeper; that there's a crawl space at the back of the cave that leads to another room. That crawl space is probably under water now. Cave rumors grow like fish stories, of course, but long caves really aren't all that uncommon in Vermont."

"How long?"

"Two thousand feet, some of them."

"Where?"

"On private property. That part is going to stay my secret."

I'm changing my opinion of the narrative qualities of geology, or at least geologists. They, too, are storytellers and are apparently not above eavesdropping. Or, for that matter, thinking about language: " 'Cave,' " says Pingree, "is a single word, but it points to a multitude of things."

As I'm beginning to see that caves are both things in themselves and a compilation of the things that may be said about them, we end up were we began: on the fast road that runs through the Intervale. Here the caves are easily seen, once you know where to look—plain as day, they look back at us with a knowing but curiously neutral expression, as if aware of our puny, temporary scrutiny.

"It's interesting," says Vince. "When you go into nature, you go out. Out of your house, out of the city, just plain out. But this isn't like that. Caves go in, and they confound all that. When you're inside a cave, you're inside nature. Like being inside a house."

We both think about the cool, dripping cavern with its abandoned nest and sculpted walls, its high window, its sense of enclosure. "A house," I tell him, "but not our house. A rock house with water. Made by water."

"And accident," Vince says.

If it is accident, it's the most elegant kind. As we watch, a hawk rises above the trees and travels down the marsh while a heron—possibly the same heron we saw before—lifts from the tall grass and travels up. The two cross almost in the middle, intent on their separate errands, apparently indifferent to the throb and smoke of humans on the road. And, I decide, indifferent to the rise and fall of ancient seas or the action of water or rocks formed near the equator.

For them, and for most human beings, the planet is cooked, finished, and will be tomorrow what it is today, though perhaps dirtier. The gassy, dead-raccoon smell of swamp comes on the breeze, and we are both suddenly grateful—to geologists, to the Winooski Valley Park District, and to the dull passage of so much time that has conspired steadily toward this moment. The heron lands in a broken tree and teeters, backpedaling its wings, and then folds itself into complete invisibility.

To get there: Take North Avenue out of Burlington toward the New North End, and turn left at the sign for Burlington High School. You can probably park in the parking lot at the high school—we did, and nobody minded. Cross North Avenue, and look for a bus shelter: about thirty feet north of it, you will see a sign and trailhead. The trail is maintained by the park district. The caves are near the north end of the marsh.

Caves can be dangerous, and the floor of this cave is both wet and mucky. Use caution, and know where you are putting your feet.

Experienced climbers may want to explore Spider Cave, which is higher on the bluff in the same vicinity. We understand it is fairly small—perhaps big enough only for a small adult or a teenager—and that it really is full of spiders. Not recommended for the squeamish or people who are nervous about heights.

Bring insect repellent, a shallow-draft boat such as a canoe or a kayak, and, if you like birds, a set of binoculars.

Indian Stones

The Captivity of Susanna Johnson

T HE FRENCH AND INDIAN WARS LASTED SEVENTY-four years and were known by four different names: King William's War, Queen Anne's War, King George's War, and, in the fourth and more or less final chapter, simply the French and Indian War. Which, to add to the muddle, is the collective name of all four wars. Because of the name, and because of the muddle, I always had an idea that the French and the Indians were fighting, which they were, but not with each other. About every three or four years I stumble over something that forces me to know something about this complicated conflict, and I go to a smart friend or a reference book and cover all that old ground again. "Yes," I sigh, "That's it. Now I remember."

I don't think my absentmindedness is unusual: We forget about this lengthy conflict at least partly because the stakes were so high. Underneath this cascade of names of

English royalty was the long struggle between the English and the French for control of North America. We look around us today and everywhere see the results of this war, and we see them as a cultural default. Most of us speak some sort of English (though an English person would argue that we don't) and live under English common law and in a hundred small ways, every day, live the outcomes of this conflict. But at the time there was no default—America was up for grabs, and America became an arena for acting out squabbles in Europe. Treaties signed in places like Ryswick, Utrecht, and Aix-la-Chapelle were mere lapses in the fighting, not resolution.

Hidden under the lumpy blanket of the French and Indian War is the peculiarly American experience of being abducted by Indians. These abductions are sometimes misunderstood to be artifacts of the long conflict between the early English settlers and the natives, and sometimes they were, but after about 1700 they had more to do with jockeying for control of the New World and with the endless bickering among European heads of state. The French enlisted the support of the Mohawk and the Abenaki to conduct a part terrorist, part commercial operation: The Native Americans would raid settlements, trash everything, and take away as many people as they could manage to ransom to the French or to replenish their own diminished supply of human beings. It's an odd constellation of events, which perhaps explains why I can never keep any of it straight.

AN ARTIFACT OF ALL THIS was the American captivity narrative, one of America's first literary genres and a cross between adventure and confessional writing, most of it unremittingly difficult to enjoy from the distance of three centuries. There's something overcooked and self-flagellating in many of these accounts—the Calvinist metaphor of hardship and redemption keeps interfering with the good stuff. Mary Rowlandson, who wrote one of the earliest and most widely published of these stories, was so busy lamenting her fate, pumping up her Christian resolve, and cataloging the cruelties of the infidel that you have to read carefully to see that her captors actually treated her pretty decently, at least by their lights. They needed to because Mary was a commodity—after eleven weeks she was ransomed home for two coats, twenty shillings, half a bushel of seed corn, and some tobacco.

THE INDIAN STONES in Reading, just south of Felchville village, stand quietly by the road and point to this era of conflict, placed there by Susanna Johnson in 1799 to commemorate her and her family's abduction in 1754 from Charlestown, New Hampshire, and the subsequent birth of her daughter on the march across Vermont. Of the two stones, at least one is not where it should be, but things often aren't—the history of on-this-spot markers that have been moved or were carelessly placed from the beginning has yet to be written, but it will probably be a long one.

The smaller stone commemorates the birth of Susanna's child: "On the 31st of August, AD 1754, Captain James Johnson had a daughter born on this spot of ground; being captivated with his whole family by the Indians." It's an entertaining use of "captivated," but only to us—in the eighteenth century the primary meaning of the word had to do with seizure and subjugation, not hypnotic pleasure. Some of us might cringe a little at the syntax that excludes the laboring mother—it does rather sound like Captain Johnson had a child born by divine agency or perhaps by mail order. And tiresome people like me object that "Captain" James Johnson was not a captain at all at the time of this child's nativity, and he wasn't a captain for very long, anyway, joining the provincial forces in 1758 and dying later that summer at Fort Ticonderoga. These are a lot of objections for a very short piece of text, but the part that is patently wrong is "on this spot of ground": Susanna intended to have the stone placed on the banks of Knapp Brook in the adjoining town of Cavendish, but for some reason her instructions were ignored.

The second, larger stone is more accurate in its vagueness: "This is near the spot the Indians camped the night after they took Mr. Johnson and family, Mr. Labarree and Farnsworth August 31, 1754; and Mrs. Johnson was delivered of a child half a mile up this brook." Then, as was traditional on gravestones, there follows a little blob of poetry: "When trouble's near the Lord is kind / He hears the captive's cry; / He can subdue the savage mind / And learn it sympathy." This is pure mayonnaise and does not rhyme, but it is probably time to stop criticizing. At least the larger stone acknowledges that it is generally women who have babies.

The glyph on the smaller stone offers a pointy and curiously formal array of weapons: bow, arrows, a tomahawk, and what looks emphatically like an ice pick. At the foot of the marker there is a small person lying in a box, like a child in a coffin. Which would make sense if the baby died, but she didn't—the child, known as Captive, grew up, married, and was the great-grandmother of Frederick Billings, one of Vermont's much-revered pioneers of environmental conservation. His home is Vermont's first, and so far, its only national park.

These are the oldest site markers in Vermont and perhaps the oldest in the nation, and age alone may account for the pictures Susanna Johnson decided to have engraved on them. For these, far more than the inscriptions, are truly arresting. On the larger marker we have a sketchy tree propped up with rifles, a lumpy human, a floating bow and arrow, and an item that might be a compass marking a heading of north-northwest or might be the force operating the bow and arrow or might be nothing at all. Under the tree, also floating, is a set of implements, one clearly a tomahawk. On the far left, as if in afterthought, is what appears to be a pair of crossed arrows, or perhaps a bird.

The picture is disjointed, evocative, and puzzling and looks like a cross between inadequate directions and an incantation. The human—shaped like a duffel bag and with a large head and tiny arms—strides purposefully among the words of the inscription; the tree flops off the edge of the picture; arrows and implements point every whichaway. The spacing of objects is more like a sentence than it is like an image, and the picture seems to stand outside the boundaries of the colonial graphic tradition.

A series of calls to the state division of historic preservation and a session in the Vermont Historical Society library tend to confirm the uniqueness of these images—there is nothing else like them either in the sepulchral tradition or, from what I can tell, in the tradition of other site markers. They may derive, indirectly, from Abenaki and Algonquin petroglyphs, and a review of the available photographs and drawings shows that they do share a flat, otherworldly, arbitrary quality. Things float in a picture plane and speak in another language, evoking shamanism. But the Indian Stones in Reading also tell some kind of story, if we can only work out what it is.

SUSANNA JOHNSON'S CAPTIVITY narrative, published about forty years after she returned home, is long-winded, polished, and full of legitimate affliction. One late-summer morning, while in the final days of pregnancy, she—along with her husband, her children, and her sister—was yanked forcibly from her bed and hurried through the forest with bleeding feet to get away before her neighbors could mount an effective response. In the opening moments of her abduction there was confusion, terror, and danger; no white settlers were killed during this particular raid, but it could easily have gone the other way. The following day Susanna went into labor, and a daughter was born on the edge of Knapp Brook. After a day of rest, the party pressed on, and Susanna was given the choice of either being left behind or riding on horseback. Horseback after childbirth is unpleasant, to say the least; the party paused about once each hour to allow her extra time to rest. Her three children, aged six, four, and two, were tired and distraught and hungry—so hungry that when the horse Susanna had been riding was killed for food, they ate too much of this unfamiliar meat and became ill. She likens the journey to a funeral procession: "The prisoners, bowed down with grief and fatigue, felt little disposition to talk; and the unevenness of the country, sometimes lying in miry plains, at others rising into steep and broken hills, rendered our passage hazardous and painful."

Still, in the course of her story, Susanna unintentionally reveals the civility of her captors and their general good intentions toward their white hostages. When her feet are bleeding after her forced march through the forest, they give her moccasins; when she goes into labor they build a shelter and, the next day, a litter for her to ride on that proves too unwieldy among thickets, swamps, and trees. She is then put on the horse, which is no fun, but is an improvement over walking, and her husband and sister are allowed to attend to her. She is permitted to rest often and eat decently, by Abenaki standards. When they reach Lake Champlain they encounter a white woman in a canoe on her way to Albany, and this woman is pressed into service to carry a message for publication in the newspapers informing their friends and relatives that they are alive. Better still, when they reach a French settlement the entire hostage party is given European food, plied with brandy, and offered a change of linen.

Upon reaching St. Francis, the Abenaki village in Canada, Susanna is adopted into the family of Joseph Louis Gill, who several times tells Susanna that he "had an English heart." As well he did: Gill was the son of two white settlers who had been abducted as children and adopted into the Abenaki tribe; these white Indians married and had seven children. Gill was blond and was known as the White Chief of the St. Francis Abenakis. Susanna either doesn't notice this about him or simply doesn't care—her mistrust of "savages" runs deep—but for forty-two days (she counted) she struggles to adapt and to make "canoes, bunks, and tumplines, which was the only occupation of the squaws."

Susanna may have been gloomy by nature, or gloom may have been thrust upon her, but gloomy she was. "Dis-

appointment and despair became well nigh being my exe-
cutioners," she writes, and added to this was the trauma of
seeing her son, Sylvanus, taken into the wilderness on a
hunting expedition. He was six, and he clung to his mother
in tears while his Abenaki master peeled back his fingers
and carried him away. It is an affecting scene, but in a matter of a few years Sylvanus will not remember it, or her, or
anything beyond his preferred life among the St. Francis.

One of the oddities of this war is that the roughest
treatment doled out during Susanna's ordeal came from
Europeans. The French, grumpy with Mr. Johnson because
of a parole violation and queasy about the progress of the
fighting, put Susanna, her husband, and her two youngest
daughters, Polly and Captive, into prison; the oldest daughter,
also named Susanna, had been adopted by a French family.
In their Montreal cell they shivered and went hungry and
suffered long bouts of anxiety and boredom. Susanna bore
another child, a boy, who, unlike Captive, promptly died. It
took two years of petitions and importunate letters for the
Johnsons to extricate themselves. In order for Susanna to
go home, she had to sail first to England and then again to
America, which proves that prisoner exchanges are not always straightforward. This one certainly went the long way
around the barn.

Susanna's story has heft, running about seventeen
thousand words, and once she started on it, it seems Susanna turned the story into a kind of life's work—the first

edition was published in 1796, and a second, "corrected
and enlarged," appeared in 1807. She was still tinkering
with the manuscript in the weeks before she died at eighty-
one in 1810, and after her death, a third edition appeared
"together with an appendix, sermons preached at her funeral and that of her mother, with sundry other interesting
narratives." Her captivity and redemption defined her and
drove her autobiography, and they brought the Indian
Stones into being in the fall of 1799.

We learn, almost in passing, that one of her daughters,
Susanna, and her son, Sylvanus, were probably more transformed by their experience than their mother. Both returned to New England reluctantly. In the space of four
years Sylvanus had essentially become Abenaki, and Susanna the younger returned only when Montreal was sur-
rendered to the English. She had been expensively and
carefully educated by her Quebecois family. "My daughter
did not know me at her return," Susanna the elder writes,
"and spoke nothing but French; my son spoke Indian; so
that my family was a mixture of nations."

THIS MIXING OF NATIONS can be painful and confusing, and
maybe somewhere in the discombobulation of the Johnson
family is the final explanation for the narrative imagery on
the Indian Stones. They try to tell a story, but it is hard to
decipher what the story really is—tree, human, bird, vec-
tor, weapons. The off-the-rack Puritan metaphor of captiv-

ity and redemption collapses, and the possibility that the stones may find some of their urgency in a Native American visual tradition is curiously pleasing. The two children, Sylvanus and Susanna, are proof of the permeability of cultural boundaries along the frontier, but it's uncomfortable proof, and we can see a mother's doubts expressed in her endless polishing of her manuscript. This may point to boredom or simple fussiness, but it more likely points to legitimate dissatisfaction. This story was Susanna's claim to fame, and she no doubt dined out on it for most of a lifetime, but it is also possible it was a story she didn't quite know what to make of.

In old age, surrounded by her children (she remarried after James died and had ten altogether), she retells the story and experiences "a kind of melancholy pleasure." I like this—her sadness is becoming, melodic, and fitting. Despite her best efforts, the Puritan mold is broken, and, like her family, there is no gluing it back together. Where else but here, by the road south of Felchville, can we listen to this fractured, worried, dramatic little song: Here was captivity and a kind of redemption but not the one she wanted. If she died without closure, then maybe she died as we all do, caught in the folds of history. It's perversely reassuring that the oldest monument of this kind in America is so complex and confusing, a working metaphor for the current century. It is melancholy. It is pleasurable. Welcome home.

To get there: The Indian Stones are on the east side of Route 106 in Reading, just north of the intersection of 106 with Knapp Brook Road. Some maps show this as Felchville Gulf Road, but don't ask me why since the sign is unambiguous. The captivity narrative can be found in Colin G. Calloway's *North Country Captives*, a 1992 compilation of abduction stories published by the University Press of New England. I'm sure it appears in other collections, but this book has a particularly thoughtful introduction.

Petroglyphs in New England are relatively rare— Algonquin and Abenaki material culture was largely perishable and portable. Rock carvings exist in Brattleboro and Bellows Falls and in various sites around Maine and New Hampshire, and at least some of these are accessible to the public.

Fireworks

Reconstructing Randolph

THE FIREWORKS DISPLAY IN RANDOLPH ATTRACTS people from all over. This year I saw license plates from Maryland, the District of Columbia, and Ohio, although I'm realistic—these good people had some other reason to come to central Vermont, some draw other than the display in Pit One of the Stock Farm. And I don't know why it's called a pit—it's a huge, open meadow bounded by woods and hills, the natural habitat of millions of fireflies. Is there a Pit Two, then a Pit Three, larger and farther down the wide dirt road that goes to Bethel?

I know people who eat dinner early to get a good slot at the fireworks; I know people who take no chances and cook dinner there. The front row at Pit One is reserved for these determined party-goers, their pickups loaded down with coolers, blankets, children, grandparents, and panting mongrel dogs with red bandannas knotted provisionally around their necks. Latecomers, like us, always envy them:

Even though the fireworks display is up there, in the sky, it's fun to watch the men working in the orange, dangerous, smoky glow; it's fun to feel close to the action. Packs of boys gravitate there like to the prow of a ship, interested in the hellish lighting and the obvious pleasure the fireworks professionals take in setup, flare, and the quick dodge backward as the rocket finally ignites.

The fireworks in Randolph are timed for the local temperament, and maybe this is why, despite the endless line to get in, and the endless line to get out, we still go every July 3. The urban model of fast, expensive, flashy displays just don't cut ice; I've timed up to three minutes between the really good chrysanthemum and the hot white sizzler that came next. It's nice: You get to watch the explosion, chart the progress of the sparks, enjoy the afterimage, and discuss whether this one was as good as the last one. "I like it when you get a good trail going up," my neighbor in a Dodge Caravan loaded down with half a dozen children tells me. "It adds to the suspense. Charlie, don't throw that halo." All the children have halos, which can be bought for two dollars at the concession stand; they rest in the tawny hair of all these sunburned children, loops of glowing blue, orange, red, and green.

"I like the kind that look over but aren't," I reply. "When you get the burst and then a pause, then the twirly things that hiss."

"Those are good," my neighbor agrees. We watch the

crescent moon, starting to dip toward the trees, and wait patiently for the next explosion.

Not everyone from out of state is entirely prepared for the leisurely pace of this. Some of them leave, frustrated and bewildered, unable to accept that our idea of excitement is not of the nonstop variety. But the rest of us prefer it, and one of the joys of the Randolph fireworks is having time to look at each other as we wander among the endless rows of cars. The fireworks light the upturned faces, and the explosions trigger two things: an echo bouncing off the hills and running down the valley and a low groan of pleasure from the multitude. The boom ricochets off the range behind us and the range over across the valley, a wild pounding that I imagine can be heard a hundred miles away. After each hot whistle, whoosh, and boom, some child begins crying. The really good fireworks, the ones that fill the entire easel of the sky, trigger applause.

It's hard to quantify why this is superior to, say, the display I grew up with on Boston's Esplanade after the Pops concert, but somehow it is. It isn't a matter of size—the turnout for Randolph is quite hefty, especially for this part of the world. Nor is it just that it's rural Vermont since lots of other towns set off fireworks, and none, in my experience, quite capture the easy tone of the Stock Farm display. It has something to do with the country music coming out of radios, something to do with the grandmothers wrapped happily in plaid blankets on the carefully laid out recliners, something to do with the studied pace of the thing. If you go, you behave well, talk to the neighbors in the cars on either side, and patronize the booth to benefit the fire department. A few years ago, as we waited peacefully to see what would happen next, we watched an elderly man with a baffled expression and a deformed shoulder wander by, and we watched with interest as he wove among the cars. Ten paces behind was a middle-aged man, obviously a son, quietly monitoring the progress of this frail creature. "Didn't want to leave him by his own," he explained to a clump of people a few cars away. While he kept his vigil, lingering at an unobtrusive distance, he arranged for the person who cuts hair to make a house call for his father early the following week—the old boy's getting shaggy again. We live in a town where barbers do that and don't charge more.

The grand finale is close to an urban model—lively and continuous and loud. The children, their faces lit by circles of hot neon, jump up and down on their high perches. "Don't wumble the sheet metal," we all scold—all over the field you can hear the groaning of car roofs as children prance on them, honking like geese, happy and distracted. We have marked another year and begun another summer, and there is celebration in the air. The last of the blue sparks drift down, and we watch them carefully, warily. Then the men sigh, start up the pickups, and we all begin to plan on a good twenty minutes of gridlock before making it back to the wide dirt road that deposits us back on paving, three miles away. A crescent moon is setting, and fireflies are everywhere.

THE WORK OF FIRE has local resonance: Starting in late December of 1991, Randolph's downtown suffered three major fires over seven months. These fires destroyed businesses and housing and the familiar outlines of our lives; the fires threatened to destroy even our communal sense of place, of continuity.

It began at about two in the afternoon on the day after Christmas in 1991. An employee in Mel's Drug heard an interesting popping sound; shortly after that, a small hot ball of flame was found cooking away behind a refrigerator. The reaction was prompt and practical: The store was evacuated in mid-transaction, so quickly that one customer apparently never got her change, and the mostly volunteer fire department was called in. The fire wasn't, at first glance, unmanageable. By the time the trucks started arriving the fire had spread up the wall to the ceiling, but "I thought we could get it out," Larry Thurston, Randolph's fire chief, told the local newspaper. Phil Mollitor, the chief of police, did notice wisps of smoke coming from around a door at the back of the building. Still, it didn't look, at the beginning, like something that would take twenty-seven hours to bring to an end.

A fire in an old building is like a cancer, and the three-story DuBois and Gay block that had dominated Depot Square since 1878 was suffering from the equivalent of a weakened immune system. Over time false ceilings, false walls, and layers of cosmetic improvements had turned the structure into an introverted maze. "My gut feeling," said Janet Stetler, who managed the drugstore and called in the alarm, "is that the fire was elsewhere. It just showed up there." Which seems, on the face of it, like an unusual thing to say: Fire is where it is. Unless, as in this case, it is also somewhere else—this fire hid itself, first in the walls, then behind thick, nauseating smoke. It finally and suddenly showed itself by shooting wildly out the front door of the drug store, a tongue of trouble, a building licking its own lips. Parched, elusive, determined, it was a fire that was spreading.

I wasn't there for this part, but I understand that things happened quickly. The thrift store, with its racks of clothes and bins of mittens, ignited with a fragrant *whoosh*, and by four in the afternoon, two hours after it had begun, the situation was clearly out of control. Or, as the Randolph Center fire chief, Albert Floyd, put it, "Things just went to hell." There were explosions—some big and some little— and as the day darkened flames began climbing into the sky. There were some reports that the fire could be seen from twenty miles away; I can confirm that the blaze was visible against the cold night sky in Bethel, the next town to the south, because that is where I saw it from, through the windshield of a moving car. I triangulated the position of the orange, smutty haze and convinced myself it was my house that was burning—homeowners do this, but this was also a period of my life when no disaster would have surprised me. Except, as it turned out, this one. And I wasn't far wrong: The DuBois and Gay block stood within a few hundred feet of my graceful Victorian, and from the south the two structures were almost perfectly aligned.

There was a certain emotional logic in coming home from a merry Christmas to find my home in ruins, but what I braced myself for and what I found contained no logic at all. From the high perch at the corner of my hilly street I saw what appeared to be a volcano erupting into the dark air at my feet—flames climbed to eye level, black smoke billowed, and tiny, sooty people climbed, shouted, and waved. It was like a Brueghel painting, complex and distracting and overpopulated; the spectators surged, eddied, and flickered in the erratic light; hoses snaked; firemen slipped and fell on the glittering rivers of ice that formed everywhere. The temperature hung around fifteen degrees. This juxtaposition of cold and dark with gold and heat had a primal and compelling beauty: I stood in thin shoes and party clothes for nearly an hour, tromping the gray, ashy snow to confirm that I had feet, unable to take my eyes away.

THAT WAS THE FIRST FIRE. It was a big one, and the Randolph community sadly surveyed the long block of frozen rubble. We took in the horrible smell, flapping our hands in front of our noses, frowning. We stood, stunned, on the ruined sidewalk, and we stared down into a hole that appeared bottomless—not because we couldn't see the bottom, but because its presence seemed inexplicable. Since the cause of the fire was still under investigation, the cellar hole seemed to be the source of some sort of mystery—also, the innards of a dead building hold a kind of ghoulish, intimate fascination. There we stood, and there some of us were still standing, when on the morning of January 27 a second major fire began in the Austin Block, a wooden Italianate commercial building a few hundred feet away.

As the smoke rose, the word in the air was *arson.*

We would have been naïve not to say it, not to think it, although it turned out it wasn't true. It felt true, or at least possible. We had to make room for the idea that someone was systematically torching the heart of our town, and it made our faces stony. We watched this fire in a kind of stupor, and the fire itself seemed to reflect something back at us: It was dense and smoky, without much in the way of drama or leaping flames. It unfolded in daylight, making it seem both more ominous and less dangerous, a tawdry and upsetting mess. We assembled and watched the proceedings, but we also muttered and examined the sidewalk. Who among us would do this, and why?

The sucker punch of the second fire was tempered only slightly by official assurances that the fire had accidental origins. It was almost surely electrical, we were told in the newspaper; it had spread quickly because, like the DuBois and Gay block, the Union Market was full of false ceilings, hollow walls, and interstices that a fire could follow, climbing upward. From the outside the building didn't look too bad, although the floors had collapsed and the roof was gone. It stood. It didn't stand for long because the owner demolished it quickly, but for a little while there was something reassuring about the uprightness of the walls.

THE BEST WAY to explain what Randolph is may be to explain what it is not. It is not a postcard Vermont village nestled around a green; it offers no handsome Georgian homes with fanlights and black shutters. That stuff lies elsewhere, at the top of the ridge in Randolph Center, which was the original town center. This newer, bigger village came with the railroad and has a railroad expression: dense, mercantile, useful, and marked by brick buildings with narrow windows, their rounded tops wearing a look of perpetual surprise. Around the downtown are turn-of-the-century neighborhoods notable largely for their variety— Italianate, Queen Anne, Eastlake, Stick, and various architectural hybrids sit on small lots behind maples and perennial borders. But the downtown also carried an air of genteel shabbiness, a slightly crumbled quality, a faint whiff of lost momentum—the upper windows in many of the larger buildings were blank and gray.

A walk down Randolph's streets before the fires was a little like visiting an older relative who fed birds and kept cats: Shops with high tin ceilings and cash registers surrounded by worn Formica carried the day. Not that it mattered—it was a place where you could buy what you really needed: food, tools, rakes, books, flea collars, clock radios, school supplies. There was even a fellow who brought in fresh fish on a truck each Friday and set up a temporary establishment near the railroad tracks, signaling to all of us the steady advent of the weekend. You could choose among three banks, visit your lawyer, pick up dinner, rent a video, and upgrade your underwear without once getting back in your car, and do it all in the context of this congenial if slightly faded glory. A friend from the suburbs of Boston marveled: "This is the way life used to be. This is the way life ought to be. I love this." That we could walk to the movie theater, pony up a few dollars, and sit with a few dozen well-behaved people eating inexpensive popcorn charmed her almost beyond reason. When the train lumbered by, shaking the building at the exact moment the lovers were kissing, she laughed out loud. "I *love* this," she said again.

Randolph, like most towns, sits on the footprint of previous disasters. A fast-moving fire consumed the largely wood downtown business district in 1884; the great flood of

1927 ripped the bridge over the river from its moorings and ate several buildings; a large mill burned in 1941, taking houses with it. There have been train derailments, and, in 1943, a B-17 crashed on Fish Hill, killing three. This is the price of continuous occupation—no matter where you park your town, you invariably get in the way of something. But this, somehow, was different. Even as the talk of arson died down, even as revitalization task forces materialized, there seemed to be an underlying queasiness. A recession troubled New England, money was scarce, and the empty lots were decidedly depressing. Randolph had a raw, exposed look, even as the ice unlocked and the spring came.

On July 4, 1992, the morning after the annual fireworks display, the town hosted its usual parade. One of the centerpieces of this procession was the eighty-five-foot ladder truck and its fire crew—the ladder was waved like a huge baton, the men and women in slickers waved and smiled, and a long cheer made its way through downtown like a tsunami. The cheering, on some sections of sidewalk, turned downright teary. This piece of firefighting equipment had been bought the previous June by Vermont Technical College and was presented to the fire district; the college has several large dormitories and was naturally worried about good protection for students on the upper floors. Nobody would have guessed that the ladder truck would see so much service so soon. Gratitude sliced through the oompah of the marching band: if there really was a firesetter in our midst, as many people still thought, then at least we had some answering gambit, some powerful chess piece, and we had people who had already engaged bravely with the opening moves of the game.

THE THIRD FIRE began four days later, on July 8, with a violent banging in some pipes: Sue Sprague, who owned the clothing store in the middle of the Main Street commercial block, heard the racket while locking up for the day. She went around the back and saw the very thing no resident of Randolph wanted to see: a finger of smoke hanging in the air behind the bank next door. Janet Kirby, the manager of the Ben Franklin department store, smelled a little smoke, called the fire department, and began crying; this quiet, desperate outburst still stands as balanced, reasonable, and sane. It didn't matter that the fire was once again small, once again apparently manageable—it once again found its way through gaps, between walls, and across ceilings. The fire was called in at around 5 PM, and by 8:30 PM it had climbed through the roof and was shooting flames twenty feet high into the lingering summer evening. By 9 PM, walls were collapsing. At 10 PM, the only item on the agenda was the desperate race to save the Red Lion Inn, a long brick building that turned the corner from Main Street onto Merchant's Row. It housed a restaurant and an auto parts store on the street level, but the real terror was that the top two floors were empty, without firewalls. If the inn went, it seemed likely that it would take what little was left of the downtown with it.

It is difficult, after all this time, to capture the still, speechless quality of the spectators, except perhaps to say that many of them sat rather than stood, and that this sitting seemed in violation of some small but important natural law about readiness in the face of disaster. I also sat, with my school-age son, and followed the firefighters' ballet—hoses, tanks, radios—with the kind of detachment that only comes with grief. If the second fire put the word arson in the air, the third made us wonder, *What now? What next?*

The Red Lion Inn did not burn, thanks to some genuine heroics, but in the space of seven months we had lost a drugstore, a real estate office, a department store, a bookstore, three clothing stores, a law office, an ice cream and sandwich shop, a bank, an insurance office, a double handful of second-floor apartments, and the thrift shop that benefited the local hospital. A restaurant and a second bank were damaged by smoke and water. Some of these businesses reopened somewhere else; some vanished.

The downtown looked and felt like a corpse, blackened and sad and unmoving, and the cellar holes were like sockets of missing teeth. Now, walking through Randolph was more than depressing; it became a funeral that refused to end. People around town had dreams. Mine consisted largely of explosions in the sky—nuclear fireworks, the final disaster—and a friend reported that she dreamed repeatedly of huge caverns opening on Main Street that revealed deadly, massive drains and lost cities of horrible people. None of these dreams defied explication, and most of them were pretty transparent, but they transcended off-the-rack anxiety dreams and pointed to a deeper wound, reopened daily, as we trudged past blackened heaps of brick with yellow plastic tape strung around the perimeter. FIRE LINE, it told us. DO NOT CROSS.

THIS STORY ENDS WELL, or I probably wouldn't be telling it. Before the ashes had cooled, the pulpits and the committees warmed: In church we were told about patience, fortitude, and joy, and in the town offices groups of citizens mobilized, using their distress as high-octane fuel for reconstruction. One of the quickest and certainly the most entertaining outcomes of this tragic energy was the decision to erect a temporary structure to house the anchor department store, Ben Franklin, until a new store could be built in the impressive hole on Main Street. This structure, with a kind of logical rigor, was placed where the now-demolished Union Market block used to be. It was made of some sort of space-age fabric that was stretched over a metal frame. The contours were white and smooth, and from across the street it looked a little like a bulbous circus tent without the stripes or, as some cheerful wag noticed, like the white silage bags that lay like benevolent worms in some of the area fields. We christened it the Ag Bag and, miraculously, began rediscovering the outlines of our daily lives.

Small-town life gets praised and vilified in roughly equal proportions in our culture: It can be constrictive, provincial, and nosy. It can also be, in literature and our imaginations, intimate and mutually supportive, driven by alliance and consensus. The truth, like most truths, is messier—some people snarled about the Ag Bag, some people were embarrassed by it, some people found it funny, and everybody shopped in it. We needed what the store offered: toys, paperbacks, fabric, winter hats, measuring cups, and spiral notebooks. The work of erecting it—done mostly by volunteers—unfolded speedily, and the new store opened with a noisy, balloon-filled party on October 24, about 150 days after Janet Kirby called in the alarm. In the meantime, construction of a new building on the site of the first fire went forward: The ground was broken on July 28, or about three weeks after the last and probably the most devastating in this string of fires.

Each person in Randolph has a story about these events, but I can tell only mine. The life of this place truly teetered and nearly fell. Some say it fell and got up again, transformed, and that might be true, but the picture in my heart is of strong arms pulling, desperately, to drag a community from the lip of an abyss. The raw labor was impressive: Volunteers fretted, argued, bargained, snapped chalk lines on pavement, lobbied for money, and examined reams of proposals and drawings. They took time away from their jobs to move dirt and look through transits, and ate early dinners to make it to long meetings held in windowless basements. And the outcome of all this activism, oddly enough, is a downtown remarkably similar to the one we had on Christmas day of 1991—a stately row of brick, a cheerful cluster of shops in Depot Square, and a surviving flat-roofed grocery store sitting in the sun. The parking is better, the sidewalks are nicer, and there are two modest parks where there were none before—one of these parks is on the old footprint of the Union Market block, past home of the Ag Bag, and it now boasts a little green space and a gazebo.

We liked what we had, and we have it again, and I find this moving. The courage to pull hard, to salvage, to strive for rightness all culminated in what might be called sameness but feels, from the inside, like graceful consistency—this kind of town and no other. Under the new buildings are scars, cellar holes, a kind of palimpsest of evil smells and bricks still smoldering, which linger like ghosts and fade slowly.

BUT THEY DO FADE. There came a time during 1996 when the fire whistle blew, and, for the first time since 1992, I felt normal anxiety, normal curiosity, normal irritation. It is a very loud, long fire whistle—it has to get the attention of a lot of scattered, otherwise occupied, volunteers. The involuntary flinch was gone, and for once I did not smell the Pavlovian fug of charred bricks or the flat, slightly metallic scent of wet ash. My stomach was fine. I mentioned this to a co-worker who lived locally, and she said she had stopped flinching a couple of months before. "I watched a big barn fire a while ago," she told me, "and it was tragic and it was scary, but it was *just a fire*." The malevolence was gone from the act of combustion.

The annual fireworks, so leisurely and so exasperating to those who do not know the temper of the town, now seem to me like a working metaphor of the townspeople's relationship with fire and each other. The deliberate pacing feels all of a piece with the rapt attention paid to stray sparks as they parachute through the trees—we know how little it takes to do an inordinate amount of damage. The lessons learned about buildings full of false surfaces may make us a little less false with each other; trial by fire has led to a tendency to savor things. Or not. I know people in town who are just as disgruntled as ever, but they seem to me to be old windbreaks against the prevailing breeze. In reconstructing sameness we have made honest change: The rebuilt downtown offers pleasant wood-and-iron benches that were not there before, and people really sit on them, as harmless as cats on porch railings, keeping an eye on passing trains, pedestrians, clouds, and stray sparks that might drift lazily through the air. Underneath this sunny lolling is appreciation and vigilance and desire, and the simple pleasure of being where you are against the odds.

To get there: The Randolph fireworks are held on July 3, with July 4 as the rain date; admission is cheap and by the carload. Take I-89 to exit 4, and then turn west on Route 66, going down the long hill toward Randolph village. Just before the village, turn left at the sign for the fireworks, and follow this road—it goes to dirt—until it's time to turn where everyone else is turning. The display begins at full dark, but the general merriment normally begins around 7:30 PM.

Randolph's central business district is on Route 12, just south of where 12 crosses the Third Branch of the White River. It's a good place to eat lunch, wander around, and maybe take in a movie—the oldest movie theater in the state is just south of the railroad tracks. The losses of the early 1990s are hardly visible now, which is sort of the whole point, but visitors can admire the gazebo that marks the grave of the Union Market and decide for themselves if this is an adequate marker. Your correspondent thinks, rather obviously, that it is.

Tales from
the Cryptozoologists

The Monster in the Lake

I GREW UP IN A STONE FARMHOUSE WITH AN ADJACENT field of weeds, and among those weeds was an old masonry springhouse that echoed like a cistern and lay low to the ground with a curious expression, mysterious and benevolent, a stone lion sleeping in the sun. I used to visit this springhouse and memorize the smell of the water—a mixture of iron and damp concrete—and I had an idea that the splashy depths of the spring were inhabited by a monster. It wasn't a particularly scary monster—I didn't think it wanted to eat me so much as avoid me—but I knew it was there. As I tromped through the goldenrod, I could hear it swirl away in the half darkness, I could feel its sudden absence on my arrival, and once I saw its long tail, thin as a whip, carve a large comma on the black surface of the water before slithering away.

I bring this up because there are people who say there

is a Loch Ness–style creature living in Lake Champlain. Like the more famous Scottish beast, he is reported to be something along the lines of an aquatic dinosaur, with a long neck and a small head and a two-man submarine-sized body. He is called Champ, and he is very shy, and he probably exists because Vermonters spend a lot of time looking at the lake and feeling a wash of romance and affection for it and because people, as a species, are predisposed to putting exotic beings in evocative bodies of water. I certainly am.

The big kahuna of water beasts is the one said to live in Loch Ness, a deep lake in central Scotland, and the first sighting dates back to the sixth century, when Saint Columba encountered the monster and soothed its spiritual turmoil. Before this encounter with Christianity the Loch Ness monster killed people and probably ate them. Though the record is unclear on this last point, it's an important one, since sustaining a creature as large as the Loch Ness monster is a hefty drain on local resources—back in 1993, *The Scottish Naturalist* reported that the lake can support only about thirty metric tons of fish, which sounds like a lot (and probably is a lot if you have to clean them), but isn't really sufficient to support a breeding population of large predators.

There are pictures of Nessie, as she is called, the most famous of which is still trotted out, despite being a known hoax. The photo was staged using a fourteen-inch toy submarine and some other handy materials to cobble up a long-necked aquatic being, and the picture was taken by a boy whose father was on assignment from a London newspaper to dig up some proof of the monster's existence. Which he did dig up, using any means necessary and with the help of his son, as this was the newspaper business and a deadline was looming. The photo, which is convincing, triggered a lot of fuss and speculation; things ballooned beyond anyone's expectations, and it seemed to the photo fakers that the path of prudence was silence. Expensive expeditions have since followed, and a kind of fascinated merriment, and a river of printer's ink. The moral of this story, if there is one, might be that a really good, resonant lie has spiritual truth in it.

Water monsters arise spontaneously wherever there is the right kind of water—a perfunctory review of the literature reveals the Manipogo, the Ogopogo, Memphre, Morag, and the Altamaha-ha, raising the question of whether Champ has a sufficiently exotic and amusing name. All these monsters have lengthy oral traditions, numerous sightings, and ambiguous, interchangeable photographs, often enhanced, in which something can been seen but it is difficult to say what. There is probably a streak of hucksterism in the monster biz, balanced by an appealing low note of earnestness—the Internet home page for Champ also frets about pollution and zebra mussels and makes rather breathless announcements about the possible use of Champ as a promotional icon for U-Haul.

There is no particular harm in the commercialization
of monsters, and, as a way of boosting tourism, it probably
does a certain amount of good. Thus Vermonters are treated
to the spectacle of a lime-green Champ cavorting on a summer lawn during the baseball season, exhorting the Montreal Expos farm team to greater victories. He can be seen
again in marble, lolling happily on the waterfront near
Burlington's rather elegant sewage treatment plant, looking
like an escapee from a children's television show. There is
Champ 101.3 on the radio dial, a Champ car wash, and no
doubt other Champ effigies that spring to life, sing a little
song, sell something, and then subside, leaving a sticky
residue.

I'm not making fun—or not a whole lot of fun—but
merely saying that these uses of Champ deflect our attention from why he is thought to exist at all. Lake Champlain is an abnormally beautiful body of water, fjordlike,
relatively clean, a slash of blue between two chains of
mountains. History has been carried on her sparkling
back—it is a place of historic naval battles, the toing and
froing of commerce, and the boundary between the Mohawk and Abenaki tribes. Rock Dunder, between Shelburne Point and Juniper Island, is said by the Abenaki to
be Odzihozo himself, the creator of land, water, and life—
he was so tickled with Lake Champlain that he decided to
settle down there and admire his work forever. It is con-
sidered good form among the Abenaki to leave offerings of

corn and tobacco on Rock Dunder. This is partly to ensure decent weather (the lake can become suddenly, horribly dangerous in a thunderstorm) and partly because even creators like to eat and smoke. The lake is deep—about four hundred feet at the deepest spot—and the surface is 436 square miles. Except for a couple of modest cities and the odd marina, the shoreline is uncluttered; this fine landscape and sparse development is clearly an ideal environment for something reticent and amazing.

CRYPTOZOOLOGY IS THE SCIENCE of animals that cannot be seen. This sounds like the premise of a Monty Python show, and, as science goes, it's serious but a little fringy— the giant squid is real, the coelacanth was a big surprise, and there are creepy crawlies in the forest that have come only recently and reluctantly to light. There's credibility there. But for a variety of reasons the more implausible and evocative creatures—Champ, Bigfoot, the South African Brain Sucker—are invariably linked to the paranormal. This happens by semantic contamination, as if ghosts, UFOs, leprechauns, Atlantis, and telekinesis are all of a piece, and of a piece with any other mystery that crosses our collective cultural path. One unseen animal, the Chupacabra, has been explained not as an invading alien in its own right but as a domestic pet the invading aliens negligently left behind—this, I understand, is from "reliable sources in Puerto Rico." Isn't that depressing? It is as if these sources, reliable or otherwise, lack a sufficient sense of trust and wonder in their own environment and must look to the skies for the answer to life's most interesting questions.

When it comes to the more metaphoric and sensational creatures, it does sometimes seem that the followers of cryptozoology miss an important point, which is that the places where hidden creatures hide is a direct function of the things that may be said or imagined about them. I think of my own beast in the stone springhouse, its thin tail disappearing into the inky water, the sunny, benevolent Champ, and the distant, rather gray femininity of whatever it is that inhabits Loch Ness, and feel that a thread runs through them. They all quietly mirror the psyches, collective and individual, of the people who live there and speak them into being. That some of these speakers are suggestible and a little sappy—an accusation I'm personally comfortable with—does not undermine the importance of local monsters staying local and inhabiting a particular place.

LAKE CHAMPLAIN IS QUITE PARTICULAR. After the Great Lakes, it is the largest body of navigable fresh water in the United States, although compared to the Great Lakes it is not much more than an impressive puddle. In 1998 President Clinton signed a bill declaring Champlain one of the Great Lakes, mostly so that Vermont and New York, which lies on the western side, could apply for Sea Grant money to do research on Champlain's health and well being. The howls of protest from the Midwest and northwestern Pennsylvania were superficially good-natured but loud and a little ham-fisted: An interviewee on public radio explained that Champlain was a "pretty good lake, but not great." It was pointed out in the same interview that a routine, medium-sized tanker from a real Great Lake would make a nifty bridge between Vermont and New York; the underlying message was that Vermont should not get uppity. All the state really wanted was the research money (which it got anyway, though the details of how escape me), but the encounter was an important lesson in how different Champlain is from the great inland seas farther west.

And it is. For one thing, the weather does not have to be particularly good to see across it, since it is only thirteen miles wide. What you see from Vermont is the high profile of the Adirondacks, including the tallest mountain in that range, Mount Marcy. Which, I hasten to add, is 5,344 feet—I can hear sniggering in Colorado and a dead, superior silence from Alaska. Vermont's highest peak is Mount Mansfield, at 4,393 feet—like the lake itself, there is something bush league in the statistics, the scale, the measurements. Which is exactly my point: The grandeur of the Champlain Valley lies in its intimacy, its perfect proportions, its sparkle. The nearness of things is part of the magic—it glitters in the national palm in a particular, faceted way. The effect is strangely hallucinogenic—when

Samuel de Champlain came here for the first time, gliding down the lake on a July morning, he claimed he saw snow on the highest peaks. He didn't, not in July, but he decided that he did. He was probably hot and thirsty. It's a telling transaction.

THERE IS A TRADITION, and a false one, that Samuel de Champlain was also the first European to report a Champ sighting. Actually, what Champlain reported was a monster in the estuary of the St. Lawrence, though it hardly matters when you think about it for a few minutes. People do see things, and there is simply no stopping them; sightings of Champ go back to at least 1819. In 1873 P. T. Barnum offered a $50,000 reward to anyone who could come up with definitive physical evidence of Champ—a corpse, a hide, anything. There were no takers, but by 1982 there were about 130 sightings and a sturdy group of Champ champions collecting evidence and wearing out their binoculars from the shoreline.

Eyewitness accounts of Champ run the gamut from unusual waves breaking on the shore to group sightings of "an animal moving along the edge of the bay" to excited reports of long necks protruding from the water in the distance. Some of these encounters are detailed and, if true, pretty astonishing—Dennis Jay Hall, one of the founders of an organization called Champ Quest, saw the beast thrashing vividly around in the shallows of Kent's Bay. Hall is the privileged author of many sightings, from necks lying on the surface of the water to bodies arching out of it to groups of monsters paddling in a flotilla down Button Bay. He is also the source of photographs of what look to the skeptic like boat wakes and floating logs, and he has had a lot of fun punching up these pictures on his computer, making them big and grainy. In truth, he enhances so strenuously that once he is done with them, they look like nothing at all. Which hardly matters—pictures of things in the water are always hard to evaluate anyway, since the scale of the image is almost always ambiguous.

But Hall is not alone: Sightings are abundant, and Champ has appeared before clumps of schoolchildren, solitary women, campers, boaters, and French Canadian tourists enjoying adult beverages on a deck. Motorists pull over and have group sightings. A Vermont nature writer, Ron Rood, gives a report of an impressive splash that woke him and his wife from a pleasant snooze in their becalmed sailboat, and he uses the encounter to consider all the possible sources of the stories of Champ—huge basking sturgeon, marching waves, rafts of waterfowl, schools of fish. In the end he dismisses all these explanations, not because they are improbable, but because they are uninteresting. "How unromantic," he decides.

Romance is important. A Champ Quester named Deuel filed a 1992 sighting of Champ from ten in the evening, when he saw a "bluish-white column of light moving to the

southwest over 0.5 miles (800 meters) away. It appeared
as if something was reflecting moonlight. It slowly followed
the New York shoreline for 20 to 30 minutes. Sometimes it
appeared as a bright flash, other times as a pinpoint of
light, and sometimes all that could be discerned was that
'something' was there. Possible moonlight reflecting off
Champ's eyes. Possibly a boat."

There's a lot of information in those last two sen-
tences—Deuel accepts that there is a less mysterious construction that can be put on the encounter, but it would be
better if this truly were moonlight reflecting off a creature's
eyes. Seen from half a mile away. On a calm, bright, and no
doubt truly lovely (if chilly) May evening. It's hard not to
wonder why Deuel didn't have something more urgent to do
that night, but I'm personally glad he didn't. Calm, moonlit
nights on Lake Champlain have certain restorative and po-
etic qualities, and it ought to be somebody's job to sit on
the shore and keep an eye on things.

Some of the sightings are downright funny. On July 9,
1992, Frank Soriano and his wife were on a drive near Bulwagga Bay, the prime and often-cited Champ hunting
grounds just south of Port Henry on the New York shore.
"While parked just south of the Pines Restaurant," says a
Champ Quest report from 1992, "[Soriano] began narrating
that maybe he would be lucky enough to videotape Champ.
He zoomed in on a seagull, he observed an animal with
his unaided eye [to th]e north, about 0.75 to 1 mile (1,200

to 1,600 m) away, moving southwest." This animal is described as "a large tree stump, larger on the bottom, round on [the top], 'like a snail's head without antennae.' " This tree stump moved "like a periscope through the water" and slowly bent over and came back up. Soriano turned the camera on the creature, which did not appear in the viewfinder but did later appear on the resulting tape.

There's a lot to like in this narration—a voiced wish to see Champ followed instantly by the opportunity to do exactly that and the evocation, in rapid succession, of a tree stump, a submarine, and a snail without antennae. A lot is happening. It is pleasing that the creature is initially invisible to technology but is somehow captured by it in the end; even a pedestrian seagull gets in on the action, and the whole story has a contingent, disorganized, curiously magical air. Unfortunately, it ends rather sadly—the folks from Champ Quest reviewed the tape Mr. Soriano took that day and determined that the animal filmed was actually a loon, but I add that a loon is a fine thing to see, film, and tell slightly unhinged stories about.

THESE SIGHTINGS—and there are lots of them—tend to illustrate why the creature in the lake is not really a monster and why he cavorts so harmlessly in the public imagination. Unlike other water beasts, he does not capsize boats, eat livestock or humans, or engage in unprovoked assaults on solitary fishermen. That would be a breach of Vermont manners—here, the integrity of individuals is prized above all other things, making the state a natural and comfortable home for artists, grumps, and oddities. Vermonters leave well enough alone. Thus Champ is not hunted with expensive submarines and depth charges; instead, in the early 1980s, both Vermont and New York passed slaphappy legislation to protect the beast from excessive meddling. There is something to be said for a place that designates *Champtanys*, a doubtful construction, as a protected species.

The emotional logic of our local monster is, like the place itself, evocative and modest, sweetly proportioned. If you go to Larrabee's Point in Shoreham to wait for the cable ferry to take you across to Ticonderoga, you can jump and wave vigorously and be seen by the boatman on the other side. If he isn't real busy, he'll be over directly—it's a manageable system that would quite possibly drive some people wild. Those of us who find this ferry system soothing can use our down time profitably looking for ammonite fossils on the windy, sunny little beach. Or looking for Champ himself—there was a sighting here in July of 1997 of an animal "approximately 15 feet long with humps"; other similar animals swam nearby. This multiplicity of Champs is consistent with recent, rather revisionist sightings in which Champ is seen with increasing frequency in the bosom of his putative family. And this is also consistent with Larrabee's Point, where roomy old brick houses sleep in the dappled shade and where the water, unlike the water in that stone springhouse so many paragraphs ago, has an appley smell, neutral and fresh, as wholesome as a turnover.

THE PROBLEM OF CHAMP, if there is one, remains happily unsolved; here is an animal that never dies, never washes up on shore, and never leaves any unambiguous traces of its existence. I will understand completely if you are exasperated that everything offered here just begs the question: Does Champ exist or doesn't he? Is there hard scientific evidence pointing toward the likelihood of large predators in Champlain, Loch Ness, or the Mzintlava River? Or is it all hokum, the dumbest story ever told?

If it's a dumb story, then it's also an important and revealing one. Redmond O'Hanlon, who served as the natural history editor of the *Times Literary Supplement*, wrote an account of his journey to central Africa to see Lake Tele and, with luck, Mokele-mbembe, a sauropod said to be living there. The book is called *No Mercy: A Journey Into the Heart of the Congo*, which conveys the idea that the author had a miserable time on this trip, and to some degree he did, but he wrestled a good deal of gloomy fun out of the adventure. The object of his quest, a creature with a neck almost as long as the oral tradition surrounding it, is treated with complicated respect by the Congolese. At one point O'Hanlon asks his guide if he himself has seen the monster. The man answers, "What a stupid question." The beast in the lake "is not an animal like a gorilla or a python," the guide explains to O'Hanlon. "It does not appear to people. It is an animal of mystery." Instead, "It exists because we imagine it."

Champ, like the Mokele-mbembe, is an animal of mystery, and he will stay in the lake as long as we continue our communal wishing of him into existence. This wishing defines a region, a temperament, a landscape, and it would be a sad day when an actual, dreary, decomposed body washed ashore. Odzihozo would not like it and might well rise from his stone chair on Rock Dunder and go elsewhere, taking the lake's sparkle and distinctive glory with him—another local god evicted from a world with no deities to spare.

To see Champ: Lake Champlain forms most of the western boundary of the state, from Benson to the Canadian border, and is thus amazingly easy to find. A review of many past sightings show that the area around the Crown Point Bridge is a prime Champ area, as are Basin Harbor and Bulwagga Bay. The sordid truth is that almost any vantage point near the water will do, and your correspondent is particularly fond of the southern, narrow end of the lake around Orwell and Shoreham. There, the lake is compressed, and so is the magic; the steep shoreline has attitude.

Button Bay State Park, which includes a natural area around Button Point, is also near many of the reported Champ sightings and, despite the small admission, is a pretty swell place. Button Bay is named for the peculiar, button-shaped clay deposits found along the shore, and Button Island is a two-acre remnant of an ancient coral reef full of fossilized marine animals. You can understand why Champ might like to hang out there. To get there from Vergennes, go mostly west on the Basin Harbor Road and then turn left at the Lake Champlain Maritime Museum. The park entrance will be on your right.

Your correspondent confesses to having forked over the admission to the Maritime Museum—a fairly rare occurrence in the life of a born-again cheapskate—and can report that this place might be worth a visit if you have cash to spare. There is a replica of Benedict Arnold's gunboat, the *Philadelphia*, some good stuff about the underwater archaeology of the lake, and a few fun exhibits where you get to press buttons, turn cranks, see movies, and monkey with computers.

The museum is open from early May through mid-October; Button Bay State Park is normally open from May through Columbus Day, with some seasonal variation. The lake is open all the time, in all weather, and does not charge anything.

Wheat Paste and Rags

The Bread and Puppet Theater

I DON'T GO TO QUAKER MEETING ANYMORE. INSTEAD, I gas up and head into Vermont's Northeast Kingdom, where the paved roads get bumpy and many of the villages take on an inward expression—half-painted, resistant, poised for flight or perhaps revolution. As I travel, I notice that the spelling of the roadside signs begins to change (FREE RABITS), that more houses come with impromptu statuary, that more of the cars look like my car, with their gray rust and subtly expired inspection stickers. On hot days dogs collapse in puddles in the road. The Kingdom, as it is called, is a place apart, provisional and defiant. This is Vermont's woodwork, a place where people and ideas lie hidden and ripen and sometimes spill out unexpectedly into dooryards.

In Glover, up the paved road that meets Vermont 16 just by the cemetery, there is an old dairy barn full of masks and huge puppets and odd paintings on cardboard:

the Bread and Puppet Museum. It sounds festive, almost childish, a school-trip destination, something trivial to do in the Kingdom on a breezy day. Puppets, right? You watch them through a little curtained opening, and they bash each other with sticks until the policeman comes. Then they bash the policemen. There's always a lot of shrieking, and sometimes the story unfolds in an unknown language, and it's all apparently about stupidity and violence on a miniature scale.

This, however, is not that. There is violence at Bread and Puppet—along with grace, worry, fitness, courage, and redemption—but none of it is miniature. Nor is this museum like any other; there are no clean surfaces, no echoing corridors. Instead, it is grubby and alarming, and you have to pause. What is this place, with its barn smells, dim spaces, and oversized inhabitants? What pack-ratty, revolutionary mind came up with this? Huge oval faces look down at you from the high rafters, wearing robes and long noses and disturbing expressions. Giant puppets loom, tall and high and watchful—you navigate in the half light through a forest of queens, demons, and huge men in porkpie hats. Goddesses challenge you with their slitted eyes, merry and enigmatic, their bodies floating thirty feet above the wooden floor. They are bigger than life, having nothing to do with life, their dimensions laid out according to the rules of an adjacent world. Long arms of old gauze end in brown hands, hands built for a hundred of our hands to hold.

Once you adjust to all the bigness, there is small-ness, too—an army of knee-high citizens occupy their chairs inside a canted bay, scattered and clustered and aligned. They fill every available thimble of their allotted space, and they look back at you placidly, like retarded children. Overhead, against the slatted ceiling of the barn, white stars with dingy bedsheet streamers smile a little ma-lignantly, but it is hard to judge, really—how, exactly, does a star smile? When you climb the wobbly stairs to the old threshing floor for the first time, clicking the lights on as you go, it's with a complacency you will very likely lose be-fore the tour is over. This is the world of gesture and old stories and a terrible stillness, packed with life.

The museum houses the hundreds, perhaps thou-sands of visionary objects created by Peter Schumann and his puppeteers, volunteers, followers, and friends since the Bread and Puppet Theater was founded in 1963. Bread and Puppet began in New York City, on the Lower East Side, and moved to Goddard College in Plainfield, Ver-mont, in 1970. Where, if I got the story right, they ran out of room and pushed on to Glover. It's unlikely the troupe could pull off another move, farther north or deeper into the hinterland—they've simply acquired too much stuff. Objects are tacked, nailed, glued, and hung from every available surface of the barn's interior so that the texture of the walls, rafters, roof planks, and bays is as packed and sculpted as the inside of an unhinged cathedral.

A cathedral, but funky and indirect. The must, the drift of decay, the scent of twenty-five winters only adds to the posed, strangely formal quality of all these creatures. The run and drape of so much fabric, the big faces uncomfortably close, are mitigated by all the dust—it reassures the visitor that nothing in here has moved lately and probably will not move today. They feel like they might, the moment your back is turned; they wear the same oblique expression you often see on volcanoes, in which stillness is the expression of a preference. As Schumann once said, the puppets are like donkeys. They don't mind not to be moved. The terrible, joyful, unrelenting, or troubling faces simply look back at you in the skimpy light, and in that exchange there is a kind of worship.

Some of the agenda is political, some of it is sort of preachy, but all of it resonates. Yes, okay, yes, good and evil. Lots of that—demons, red and swirling and decked out in vermilion rags; herds of sweet, wise deer with twiggy antlers; bad men with thick necks and piggy expressions; oppressed women with kerchiefs on their heads. But the morality play is more complicated than that: Each puppet also seems like a refugee from the land of myths and dreams, offering in its big hands the key that is also a door that is also a bone. It's confusing, and more than a little disconcerting. Schumann, in his 1989 essay "Subversive Museum," enfolded in a queer little red booklet about the place, captures this when he writes, "During rehearsals of our puppet shows we often get stopped by this self-instilled life of objects. They don't want to. We want. But when we look them straight in the eye, they say 'no' more often than not. And this impasse is an education; it suggests a possible reign of silence."

I feel this silence: I like to go when the barn is likely to be empty. I pick a weekday morning, perhaps a chilly one, and go stand and look, caught up with what can be done with paper, flour, and a few rags. *Low tech* is not quite the word for this kind of theater; *no tech* is probably closer to the truth. Old shoes from the thrift shop, rusty chairs, bottle caps, acres of ancient fabric and poster paint. Small signs here and there explain, or fail to explain, the origin of these obsessive and expressive creations: "Cruciform puppets," says one, "1963, from many different Easter plays which we played in many different churches in N.Y.C. through the 60ies mostly as allegories of political pain. The ceiling is the left over from the Vermont papier-mache cathedral at Cate Farm where most of the wheat paste figures got eaten by mice." I like the tone of this and the implicit acceptance that mice must eat and the look of these leftovers, these saints on the ceiling. Mud people, reclining and stretching, sitting and walking—it's reassuring, this art without craftsmanship, this acceptance of decay.

But behind this acceptance of death is an urge for newness and abundance—there are so *many*, and they are always making *more*. Hundreds of little cardboard squares painted with worrisome chairs or bas-reliefs in a series stretching thirty feet along a partition, a temper tantrum of emerging figures, doors open and closed, verbal fretting about injustice, lots of muddy black paint. The final panel, exhausted, mutters, "The system is unmanageable."

As if sheer volume were not enough, there is something unnerving about the human curviness of all these faces, all these bodies, all these huge, pointing hands. For it is about people in their poses and expressions, about the masks of people, about the almond eyes and molded cheekbones, the bodies like dough, expressive and indelicate. There is clumsiness, a lack of apology, an unwillingness to compromise, so that even the animals look back at you with human eyes, their round irises in queasy contrast with their equine noses. I have seen visitors step back involuntarily, while others step forward. Either you like it very much or you do not like it at all.

THROUGH THE SUMMER OF 1998, the puppet makers in Glover would pull out all the stops once a year and call us home to Our Domestic Resurrection Circus. This two-day event was a celebration of banners, dust, bread, drums, and the spicy scent of each other in the buttery Vermont sunshine. Up to sixty thousand people came to the big field and the grassed-over-gravel-pit amphitheater across the road from the museum. That's a lot of people, and it mystified me, for many years, how so many of us could congre-

gate and create no traffic jam, no bottlenecks, no parking
problems. There were problems, of course, with foot traffic
in the road and litter and heatstroke and beer, but there
was something in the open weave of the event, the abundance of things to do once you got there, and the resiliency
of the congregation, that made most of us leave our impa-
tience at the door. There were sideshows and the Circus,
the rehearsal for the Pageant and the Pageant itself, and
passion plays well into the night. People came when they
wanted and left when they were done; this was a crowd in-
capable of surges.

Just the titles of the sideshows give the feel of the
thing: In the resiny cool woods we sometimes heard "The
Seven Last Words of Christ" (I was too far away to hear
what they were, but the Haydn carried), "All About Sleep,"
and "A Warning to Other Crows." Some were noisy, some
were quiet, and they all had a way of emptying you, teaching you to wait. Soldiers came to villages, birds descended,
mirrors flickered on burlap curtains, and a handful of tiny
brown men would fold and unfold a set of triangles in silence, explaining something important about edges and
color. The puppeteers milked cows and advanced argu-
ments. Marriages and funerals arose spontaneously, while
men with big heads shifted furniture and sent for the doctor. It was not, in any conventional sense, entertainment,
but it held the attention in a firm but ambiguous grip.

The afternoon Circus was a circus, with the breathless, distractible quality a good circus should have: the band of white-clad musician-puppeteers wheezed and thumped their way through "You Are My Sunshine," provided the required fanfares and drum rolls, and joined the merriment when extra turbulence was required. Beasts were tamed, tigers jumped through flaming hoops; there were dragons and baboons and horses. There was everything a circus evokes, except these were performers decked in wearable puppets, out of scale, odd, convincing. And the politics were everywhere—one summer we laughed and booed as Oliver North "cannonized" Hillary Clinton, Barbra Streisand, Bernie Sanders, and "the homosexual who does my wife's hair, I hate that guy." The celebrities were called down from the audience, the fuses were lit, and each in turn was shot in a high tumbling arc into oblivion, only to reappear on the roof of the nearby bread house, jeering. *Nah nah, didn't work, nah nah.* Barbra minced and primped, Hillary swung her briefcase, the hairdresser displayed some impressive tattoos, and Bernie Sanders, Vermont's lone congressman and an avowed socialist, needed no theatrical exaggeration—the rumpled shirt and earnest body language were really his, proving there is still plenty of room in politics for good humor. We cheered, he gave a modest politician's wave, and the show went on.

Underneath the oompah-pah ran a dark-green streak of myth—we may get Oedipus Rex in four and half minutes, but it is Oedipus Rex nevertheless; we may get a huge, sad woman we cannot identify who shows us the contents of a suitcase; we may get a slow dance from Machu Picchu. Then, without pause, a bevy of children on stilts or grasshoppers on bicycles or a cheerful little war between the plutocrats and the downtrodden that will likely end in a dunking. These vignettes from the other side were a kind of fair warning: If you didn't like them, plan to leave before the end of the afternoon, before the serious story-telling began.

The evening Pageant opened just as the first note of dusk was falling, in that precise moment when the air thickens like ink dissolving in a glass of water. It was always, in some sense, the same: A tall goddess assumed the ground, benign, beflowered, large, and safe, and attended by puppeteers who seemed curiously detached, respectful, stiff. They manipulated her solemnly; a circle was formed, and a song was sung. This was the last of the human voice we could expect to hear for a while—the Pageant had noise, but no speech. Instead, we got an unfolding, a juxtaposition, a series of convergences. Each year I was startled by the newness of this ancient tale, the one in which the Bad Stuff comes and ruins everything, the one in which our efforts are all compromises, the story of loss, unsteadiness, and, after the manipulations of courage, redemption. The Pageant drew me into the world of slow-moving, terrifying collisions between weeping, elongated women and the slice of the guillotine, between sweet sheep and advancing slaughter, between a huge, headless suit and a bevy of folks with fragile brooms.

The Pageant changed from year to year but always resolved itself in the same way. At the end was fire—we always got to burn something, always the Bad Thing, and the fire was lit by the huge Mother Earth figure that took forever to arrive, manipulated by a hundred puppeteers and volunteers. She came over the hill as the exact and final answer to the pretty, pastoral creature we began with—not flowers but dirt, the dirt that sustains us and demands our allegiance. Dirt and fire and the collective sigh of thousands of people as the object of our communal fear and hate ignited. The puppets withdrew and we advanced, watching the flames and the floating ash and daring to rejoice. We looked at each other. Something had happened. The moon lifted.

IN THE PINE WOODS on the Circus grounds is a sort of village, little Ewok houses dedicated to dead puppeteers and friends. Inside these houses, which you must duck to enter and are never bigger across than you can reach with your two arms, are peaceful, unsentimental objects related to the person's life. In one, things bong and ding when you touch them; in another, the hubcap of a beloved Volkswagen Beetle rusts in a corner.

Children like them—they wriggle with pleasure at these clubhouses exactly their size; they look and climb and wish they had one like it at home. It never troubles them much that it's a kind of cemetery, although it's obvious to all but the toddlers that this is what it is. "He must have been nice," my son reports to me about the tall, narrow house with little more than a faded picture and a three-legged stool inside. "They gave him a high window." I walk around to the side and see that he's right—up there like the tip of a homemade periscope is an opening that catches air and light. This explains something. I feel real loss, real affection, and a dollop of envy—he had friends as good as these, friends who built this, friends who would not settle for an empty marker.

This village of dead friends has taken on an unplanned resonance. In 1998 death itself visited the annual Circus, and perhaps, in retrospect, we all ought to have seen it coming. And perhaps some people did, because, as the event matured, people seemed a little more hesitant about bringing their young children. On August 9, Joshua Nault, twenty-two, of Morrisville, got himself overstimulated on drugs or alcohol (or perhaps both) and began acting up in a campground not far from the farm. According to witnesses, Nault was kicking things, calling out, and spoiling for a fight; and so Michael Sarazin, forty-one, of Post Mills, interceded and tried to get Nault to calm down. This, Sarazin explained, is not what we do here. Nault allegedly hit Sarazin on the head, killing him, thereby effectively ending more than twenty years of pageantry in Glover.

This death was a symptom and not, as some think, a cause. As the years progressed, the annual event had drawn more and more people interested primarily in taking drugs and staring in a vacant and puzzled way at things bigger and more important than a television. There had been overdoses and disagreements and illegal transactions, to say nothing of a couple of memorable dogfights. On the periphery, things were clearly headed in a strange direction. Despite repeated requests from the puppeteers to leave dogs and drugs at home, Our Domestic Resurrection Circus had suffered a kind of slippage. With its recurring insistence on the importance of overcoming tyranny, it had attracted a fringe of lawlessness, which is not the same thing, but the distinction is difficult to frame when talking to a drunkard.

Grief and alarm accompanied the events of 1998, proving conclusively what we already know: Nobody likes change. But there is durability here, and compromise, like a gesture in a night play we have seen before. The end of the annual Circus marks the beginning of something else, perhaps something more effective and subversive. This kind of storytelling is about individuals, about personal and political change, about participation. Over the years I have volunteered to run with flags, sing songs, and sweat mightily behind a papier-mâché wall of weeping women, all props to the larger Bread and Puppet action. The plan now is to offer smaller performances, more intimacy, more opportunities for discomfort. The Circus is not going to go away, but it may well fracture into smaller pieces, manageable and insidious.

THE BREAD PART of Bread and Puppet has the overtones of sacrament but is at once simpler and more complicated. The idea, as I understand it, is that there is a false separation between one kind of food and another—we need both bread and puppets, and for the same reason: We are hungry. On Circus day, people would line up peacefully for a taste of the rough homemade bread, not because it tasted particularly good—because it didn't—but because of the ceremonial quality of the line, the wait, the dry sourdough, and the queer garlicky butter. Bread is a way of remembering that plain food is rare and our stomachs should be filled—no matter that we would all return to our coolers and blankets and crack out the chips. The length of the line and the body language of the people in it said a great deal about the muscle behind this idea. They stood like sleepwalkers, holding time but not using it, place holding, but not merely waiting. There was a positive quality to it. They looked like sweet creatures paired before an Ark, or like something in a corner rafter of the barn.

For some, the Bread and Puppet experience is uneasy. They come to the performance or to the museum with friends, inadequately prepared, hopeful for something new. But there is a problem: Art, for many, is about finished edges and little captions and distanced interpretation over plastic cups of wine. This is a mess, this comes too close, plus it smells funny, with the sweet reek of dust and time, ripe outhouses, and fresh pesto. You can read their faces and see that there is nothing here for them to fall back on. "What's she doing?" they want to know as the antler girl carefully cooks an egg; "What *happened*?" they ask as the dancers tear apart the totem. It's an assemblage of junk and weirdness, and it won't cross over. "I want to go back," they say. They chew the bread sadly, unsure about what is being asked of them. LIGHT DEATH WATER, say banners on poles tall enough to string electricity, BREAD SISTER AH. "Can we go *home* now?" But we are home, and there is no other.

BACK IN THE MUSEUM, alone on a chilly August morning, I feel a corner of their discomfort creep into my own heart—it's all so downwardly mobile, so challenging, at times even tiresome. Go away, white horse, go away, butchers. Bleached peasants with wooden blocks for feet sprawl next to a woman endlessly kneading bread in a rough bowl gouged from the stomach of a tree; out a window in a lower gallery I can see the side of a newer building, board-and-batten, with narrow and reiterative black figures like petroglyphs dancing, and it does seem that there is an obsessiveness veering into madness here. More tiny pictures, more massive hands, more chairs, more doors, more stories. It's anxious, and the anxiety is contagious. If I nurse it, it will bloom into terror. But if I leave it alone, which has always been my inclination anyway, some blank and wordless part of me takes over and manipulates the world of Peter Schumann with something approaching confidence or at least acceptance. The nightmares stand here so stubbornly so that we might recognize them and eat. They taste like bread, a little dismal and nutritious. Those high, white stars still trouble me, and the puppet faces still seem close, huge, impossible, but in their presence I let go of all my smugness, something I am better off without. A plump, healthy woman who I later realize is Schumann's wife, Elka, approaches me, asks if she can help. "Yes," I tell her, and we look at each other until suddenly we both laugh. "I'm sorry," I say, "it seemed like a good answer. The right thing to say." She shrugs, still smiling, and dematerializes in the dust and gloom, and the puppets watch her go with many eyes, my eyes, the eyes of animals.

To get there: Take Route 2 east from Montpelier to Route 15. In Hardwick, pick up Route 16, and turn right on Route 122. The museum is on your left. Be thoughtful about where you park; don't block the road. The museum is open daily from 10 to 6, May to October, and it is often unattended. Put a small donation in the can and wear sensible shoes—the old barn floors are quite uneven.

Performances are often underpublicized: low-profile newspaper listings seem to get the job done. This Web page will also help you get oriented to the odd mix of Marxism and myth that the troupe offers. The puppeteers also travel quite a lot, and there can be long gaps between performances. The museum, however, requires only minimal planning and does not seem to go anywhere, although it does, which is why it is a good museum.

A Very '70s Thing to Do
Abstractions on the Interstate

LIKE A LOT OF BABY BOOMERS, MY EARLIEST memories are of long car trips. This was in the days before seat belts, and we rattled around in the back and poked each other with small but sadistic fingers, and once, rather memorably, I threw my brother's Little League hat out the window. He surprised us all by bursting into tears, and we petitioned the grown-ups to go back for it. Which they refused to do—we had time to make up if we were going to be in Philadelphia before dark. I have an idea that these kinds of memories are widespread and interchangeable, as if an entire generation was raised in the back of a moving station wagon, inhaling dog hair and eating potato chips.

Rest stops are part of the gestalt: vending machines, water fountains, sour-smelling bathrooms with strips of damp tissue on the floor, a foyer with black-and-white floor tile like a huge chessboard, and a map screwed to the wall

behind a sheet of glass. Outside there were always heavy
picnic tables painted brown, vaguely sticky, often tippy despite their heft. I evoke the American rest area with the
blended memories of a thousand encounters, and I can see
you, the reader, nodding. Yes, you say, I remember that.

What I don't remember is sculpture, and neither do
you. But there is some—actually quite a lot of it—along Interstate 89 in Vermont, made from local marble and poured
concrete. These sculptures sleep in the snow and bake in
the sun and, like the rest of us, get steadily older and sor-
rier. And more invisible—we live in a culture of the new.

I always knew about one of the sculptures—it's visible just past the Stowe exit when you are heading north. I
add quickly and with a dash of shame that for all those
years it never crossed my mind that what I was noticing
might be art. I thought it had something to do with echoes.

The statue hovers over a rest area like a huge ice-
cream scoop stuck in the ground. The bowl of the scoop
faces out across the valley with a functional expression,
similar to what you see on a satellite dish. Because of this
functional expression, and because I have logged a lot of
hours at those hands-on, kids-only science museums, I had
an idea that this big scoop collected some sort of special
noise or signal from the hills above Waterbury and did
something with it—amplified it, bounced it, converted it to
rare gases, or maybe turned it into candy. If I stopped,
there would be some sort of explanation and a set of direc-

tions, neatly bolted to the base behind a sheet of cloudy Plexiglas.

One day not long ago I did stop, for some perfectly good automotive reason. That may have been the day my 1985 Subaru started pulling badly to the right or the other day when I thought it might finally have set itself on fire— I can't remember, which says a lot about the kinds of cars I drive. While waiting for the damage to heal, I climbed the little hill that the scoop sits on to take a closer look.

The thing stands about fifteen feet high and is made out of concrete; it's in rough shape and the rebar is starting to show. It has a square base, a curving handle, and a bowl big enough to sit in if you don't mind bumping your head. In this bowl I saw that someone had recently set a candle, which had burned down to a puddle. There was some writing inside of the usual sort (Jack plus Cary; sexual instructions) but no writing on the outside explaining what, exactly, this thing was. I looked across the valley for the radio tower, the thin red laser beam, perhaps a corresponding concrete sousaphone on the other side of the highway. There was nothing—only the calm green hills and the hum of traffic and a few of those cotton-wool clouds that keep turning into animals.

DICK FOSTER, the statewide Information Center director who is overseeing the rest stops these days, explained that the art on the interstate was placed there through the efforts of Paul Aschenbach, who was on the faculty at the University of Vermont. All the pieces were made and placed during a period of creative frenzy in the late sixties and early seventies. "Done, I think, over two summers."

"What?" I said.

"Oh yes," he said. "It happened fast, and there are a lot of them. By famous people, too." He paused. "They aren't in very good condition, I'm afraid."

"How many is a lot?"

I could hear him counting in his head. "Sixteen or seventeen. At least fifteen. They are all along I-89, and on I-91 south of White River Junction. Most of them are set back, so you can't really see them from the road."

He referred me to Ann Lawless, who was once the coordinator for Vermont Save Outdoor Sculpture. In 1993 Lawless and Vermont SOS conducted a survey of public sculpture around the state, and the interstate art naturally came under review. "Paul Aschenbach organized two symposiums back in the late sixties, early seventies," she told me, "with sculptors from around the world who were personally committed to the idea of public art. They made the pieces and, with permission, installed them up and down the interstate so people could enjoy them."

"This sounds expensive. Where did the money come from?"

"No idea. Vermont Council on the Arts, maybe?"

"What did the survey say?"

"That concrete is probably not the best material for statuary if you can't maintain it. No big surprises there."

"It looks bad?"

"Some of the pieces are okay, some are pretty tragic."

"What's this business about a symposium?" I have a primitive imagination and kept imagining men in togas drinking wine and reclining on couches.

"A symposium brings sculptors together to work on a short-term project, along with apprentices and interns. They came and spent one summer, back in the late sixties, and came back for another summer in the early seventies. They made a bunch of outdoor pieces, and arranged with the federal and state highway people to put them in the rest areas. The idea was that art should be public, it should be set up in public places, that we need more art in our ordinary lives."

Which is true. As I hung up the telephone, I revisited, with nostalgia, the idealism and pushiness of art back then. It was an idealistic, pushy age, and suddenly it became urgent for me to go and take a firsthand look, which proved alarmingly easy. I live near Interstate 89, and three of the pieces are at rest areas less than ten miles from my house. I am embarrassed by this ease—how can you live someplace as long as I have without knowing something of its riches? The answer also embarrasses me. Truth be told, it never even crossed my mind to look for art as I drove too fast to Montpelier to get somewhere before it closed already.

And, in my defense, the sculptures—except for the ice-cream scoop—are almost always at some distance from the road, away from the hissing tires and the roadkill and the big green signs. In Randolph, at the southbound exit, the sculptures are even squirreled away in a designated scenic area, tucked in behind the rest area buildings in a little park.

Here are the familiar brown picnic tables and the big green trash barrels and two of the sculptures. One is busily evoking gears and machinery. It has a distinct downhill cant—it was installed in a grassy glen, and it looks like the ground underneath it has subsided quite a lot over the past thirty years. This saddens me, and the sculpture saddens me, though I can see that in a seventies way it's not a bad effort: a heavy turntable and a muscular arm seem to invoke that icon of the times, the record player. The surfaces are pebbly and brutal, conjuring up skinned knees and Bactine. Over in the trees is another effort, an arrangement of textured marble blocks we are probably supposed to climb on; the back of the sculpture forms an enclosure, a kind of hideout, and from here you can peer through a slot at a sign. "Tune your radio to 90.1 FM for current travel and tourist information," it tells me.

I wander back and forth between these two artifacts, and look at the sign, and at a family of four eating a solemn lunch of sandwiches. Randolph is a high, windy place, and a wrapper blows, scudding across the pavement and fetching up against some birches. A woman about my age goes to retrieve it and winds past the sculpture in the trees. She does not seem to see it, and it does not seem to see her, either. It sits in the trees, blank and aloof and apart from life's conversation.

This first encounter troubles me a little, and I want to see more. I spend a few days cruising the interstate and looking at statues and noticing the earnestness emanating from them, along with a visionary desire to instruct and inform. The works wobble from the pointy and geometric to the lumpy and heroic—some are bones in the ground, some are controlled explosions, some are mute slabs of feeling. The problem with them, I realize, is not that they are bad art so much as art that has gone out of fashion. Someday they will perhaps come back in, and their weighty, textured surfaces will engage us again.

IF THEY LAST THAT LONG. There are real logistical problems with the art on the interstate, and real questions about their history and our cultural values. I call Dick Foster again; he has worked with the Department of Transportation for more than twenty years, and he sees the sculpture problem as a series of urgent questions with no answers. "It's very difficult," he tells me over the phone. "These statues have no constituency. They aren't like the monument on the green that people walk by on their way downtown every day. Nobody loves them in that personal, community way." And, he points out, at least one of the statues is nearing a crisis:

Its rest area must be closed and the site leveled. The sewage system is failing, the concrete of the piece is crumbling, and there is no clear, right thing to do. "Even if we had the money to move it," he tells me, "it's very deteriorated. It might fall to pieces." I can tell by the way he says this that the whole business troubles him—our ideas about art make us treasure it, but the reality of this art is that it is a nuisance.

I go back to driving the interstate, racking up hundreds of miles to visit these sculptures again. The ones of stone, I realize, have weathered thirty years of snow and wind better than the ones of concrete, but all have a battered and neglected look. The offering at the Sharon rest area began as heroic stepping stones, stacked to form an oversized staircase, but merrymakers have since tampered with it, turning the huge concrete slabs off square. It must have been massively difficult to do—at least four people had to have been in on the prank, along with an unspecified quantity of alcohol. I can't decide if this troubles me or not, but I do decide that the lopsidedness is now a part of the history of the piece, and a comment on it, and a way of thinking about it. These abstract statues, it is true, do not stir the emotions like the doughboy on the village green, but they stir up *something*, and here is the aftermath.

A FEW WEEKS after my love affair with the abstract art on the Vermont interstate has cooled, I suddenly acquire a book about the two sculpture symposiums. In it I learn the mechanics of the thing—it was supported through a partnership of the National Endowment for the Arts, the Vermont Council on the Arts, the Vermont Marble Company, S. T. Griswold and Company, the Episcopal Diocese, Dayton Sure-Grip East, and the Vermont State Department of Highways. Over the two summers that the project was in full swing about $70,000 was spent, which strikes me as a lot of art for a modest investment. I examine this budget closely—nobody, including the artists, got paid. Or got paid much more than squat: about $37,000 was spent on supplies, about $1,200 on wages and salaries, and the rest on getting the artists to Vermont and keeping them fed. The book offers arty, full-bleed, black-and-white halftones of each piece, all looking prim and new, and a map of where each piece is located on I-89 and I-91. I notice with some dismay that the map is inaccurate—Sharon is not north of Brookfield—but it's instructional in a way I hadn't anticipated. The map shows the variety, the briskness, the intent of the enterprise, and it restores my faith, which was shaken, in the idea of modern art in public spaces.

I CALL UP DICK FOSTER again; I'm becoming a pest, and I know it, but he does not seem particularly grumpy.

"It says in the symposium materials that the sculptures are for sale. Are they?"

"No," he says. "Well, no, probably not. I don't think
so. That was the original idea, but once they were all installed, they became the property of the state. I think. I
don't know. If they were for sale, they'd be the dickens to
move.

"Still," he adds, "I wish somebody would care about
them—if people want to do something about them, then
now is the time to act."

Action, I realize as we talk, is an important part of the
sculptures' history—in two short summers (and the summers are short around here) a great deal of energy was ex-
pended to put these objects in the public domain. It's
admirable, I tell myself, but is it art? Such a subjective,
unanswerable question. I make a mental inventory of the
pieces, and I confess that I sometimes found myself more
interested in the vines growing over a sculpture than in its
original, impenetrable message. In one rest area the work
sits next to the Dumpster, and these two objects converse
surprisingly well across a chasm of time and intention.

"Is it art?" I ask Foster.

He would prefer not to answer but tells me there are
some people who think it would be best to simply demolish
the most decayed sculptures and be done with it. We share
our mixed feelings about this idea—they are a problem,
but they don't deserve this kind of expedient solution.

"Is it art?" Foster asks me.

"I don't know," I sigh, also preferring not to answer. "I

don't know what it is. It's there, and it tells a story, and it was certainly a very seventies thing to do."

I'M BACK AT WHAT SURVEYORS call the point and place of beginning, gazing up at an ice-cream scoop that I once thought had something to do with echoes. Which it does, but not in the way I had imagined. It looks different to me now. I notice that, in spite of sitting on what appears to be ledge, the sculpture is tipped a few degrees and has a defeated, neglected air. It looks smaller than it did at first, less functional and more vulnerable. I consider taking it home and am made droopy by the logistics of moving it. Plus the neighbors would freak, and it might collect rainwater and breed mosquitoes. But I want to, and recognize this urge as healthy—it's the same urge I always had when I saw a Victorian house being demolished, back in the days when the word *Victorian* was permanently wedded to the word *monstrosity*. Which does not seem so very long ago— about the same time, I realize, that this oddity was created and placed here, looking forever at the fragrant hills above Waterbury. Now, the Victorians have had their revenge, and we restore their houses lovingly, cooing over vergeboards and spindle work and fish-scale shingles, and we admit these houses as ambassadors of history. A lot of Victorian houses did get bulldozed before that happened, and perhaps some of these sculptures will also die of neglect or even hostility, but I hope not. I can't take this one home, but I can stand here and acknowledge it, and I can take a few clumsy photographs.

As I do, a man in his twenties watches me and then approaches; even in Vermont women should not talk to men in rest areas, but he seems harmless enough.

"I've often wondered," he says to me. "What is that thing?"

"What does it look like to you?"

"Some kind of monument?" he asks. "Did something happen here?"

Something did, I realize, and I like this answer. We look up at the enormous spoon, and I explain that there is art everywhere, all up and down the interstate. I give him a short version of how it got there.

"I've lived here all my life," he says, "and I never knew that." He grins, and I find I am grinning back. "That's pretty good," he says—but not, I think, to me. "That's quite an idea. That's decent."

To get there: The sculptures can be found in the rest areas on northbound I-91 in Guilford, Putney, Springfield, and Hartland and on southbound I-91 in Hartland and Putney. Northbound I-89 has sculpture at the rest areas in Sharon, Randolph, Waterbury, Williston, and St. Albans and southbound I-89 has pieces in St. Albans/Fairfax, Williston, Waterbury, Randolph, and Sharon. The Randolph southbound exit has two.

As the above story mentions, perhaps once too often, the sculptures seem to need less of our indifference and more of our attention—they are things both to be seen and appreciated for what they are and a problem to be solved. Intelligent ideas can be forwarded to the Vermont Department of Buildings and General Services, 134 State Street, Montpelier, VT 05601.

The Demands of Heaven

Aspet and Augustus
Saint-Gaudens

NEW HAMPSHIRE HAS NO SALES TAX, AND THRIFTY
Vermonters on the eastern side of the Green
Mountains often drive to the West Lebanon miracle mile, a quarter inch over the state line, to buy what
they need. Shoes, clothes, food, books, even fancy bed
linen and upscale coffee, all without the surcharge. We
are supposed to declare this unpaid sales tax to the Vermont government each April and hand over what we
haven't paid, but nobody does it. Instead, we take our meager rebates from Montpelier, cross the Connecticut River,
and blow the money on tax-free CDs, blue jeans, and perhaps even a seafood dinner at the Weathervane. Here,
they keep their overhead low by serving everything on paper plates, so there is a festive, picnicky quality to the
place—the New Hampshire state motto, Live Free or Die,
might as well have a subhead that says Eat Cheap.

Along the miracle mile, mixed in with the sign clutter for the Carpet Barn and the Home Center and McDonald's, is a brown rectangle announcing the Saint-Gaudens National Historic Site. I lived here for more than five years before I stopped believing this had something to do with the Catholics. It sounded like a shrine, and I pictured red carpeting, dark arches, shrunken relics, plaster saints. Then one day somebody told me that Augustus Saint-Gaudens was responsible for the Lincoln Memorial in Washington, that mammoth and oddly casual portrait that is best seen at night. The name took on context; my curiosity was aroused; I have a certain affection for this particular piece of oversized, patriotic statuary. It looks for all the world like the great man is sneaking an after-hours read, hiding his novel whenever someone comes around the corner. He looks comfortable, ugly, a marble giant in a marble giant chair.

But it isn't true. Saint-Gaudens did not do the Lincoln Memorial. He did the Lincoln in Lincoln Park in Chicago, which I have never even seen. No matter: The error worked, since it called me under false pretenses down to Aspet.

Aspet is Saint-Gaudens's home, in Cornish, New Hampshire; it is about twelve miles south of the commercial strip, at the end of a winding, shady access road. There is a booth at the end of this road where money is handed over; for this fee you can wander freely through the high-hedged outdoor rooms with carefully placed statuary, admire the

complicated, fussy gardens, visit his studio, and tour a portion of the house guided by a knowledgeable employee of
the National Park Service. Instead of flush toilets, the public is invited to use a composting toilet just off the parking
lot that comes with a lot of instructions—this is somehow
in keeping with the extreme tidiness of the place, the acres
of grass that appear to have been scissor-trimmed by elves,
the smooth topiary walls that make the outdoors here so intimate. During the summer, concerts grace the grounds—
brass quintets, piano duets, recitals of flute and piano—and
in a separate building called the Picture Gallery, there are
showings of contemporary art. It's nice.

I am allergic to nice, and it took a while for me to figure out why the place has such appeal, why I needed to go
back so often. I have always preferred messiness and slop
and excess of temperament, and the restrained and tidy
look of the place ought to give me the willies. Sometimes
it does. But still I go back, as if the place has asked me a
question I can't answer. Each time I go, I pause and really
read the literature, badly printed on cheap paper, and follow the neat hedges twice as tall as I am, and generally do
what is expected of a visitor; and each time I go away happy
but unsatisfied.

This welcome feeling of unrest might have something
to do with the house itself, which does not wish to be seen.
It hides behind high horseshoe-shaped hedges that are so
dense and so perfectly groomed that children are lured in

among the roots, perhaps never to be seen again. After using the clever toilet, you follow the curve of these scissored trees with the full expectation that the path just keeps on curving and deposits you back in the dust of the road and the parking lot, blinking sadly at the man who took your money. But no, here is the break, a brick herringbone path that leads upward; here is a large, rather sickly tree that is dying by inches near the door. The idea, obviously, is to keep you from seeing the whole house, whole, with its stepped gables, its overweight facade, its mournful mullions in the windows. Later additions and changes have added a grace note to the proceedings, but the house in its basic form is as heavy and as tasteless as a load of dough.

Saint-Gaudens first saw the house in 1885, only four years after his first major commission, the Farragut Memorial. He was thirty-seven, a sculptor on the rise, and his trained eye naturally found the place bleak and depressing—the month was April, when all of northern New England is bleak and depressing, and the house did not help matters along. Then, it was much more exposed to the eye and the weather, and the proportions—despite the later horticultural distractions—are still lumbering and dull: bigness without elegance. There is a story, recounted in the flyer, that his wife, Augusta, insisted the place would look all right once spring really came. Which it probably didn't, but the clincher was that the owner, Charles Beaman, said Saint-Gaudens would find plenty of craggy Yankees in the district who would aid him in his work on a statue of Lincoln that he was making for a park in Chicago. Art first, comfort later.

He called the house Aspet, after the village in the Pyrenees where his father, a shoemaker, was born. Saint-Gaudens himself was born in Dublin in 1848, during the Potato Famine, and like many Dubliners of his generation he actually grew up in New York. The place in Cornish did get the sculptor away from the heat and bad smells of the city, and he worked to mediate the brooding look of the place by adding, subtracting, multiplying, and dividing. He pasted on columns and gables and porches until one friend described it as "an upright New England farmer with a new set of false teeth" and another as "some severe and recalcitrant New England old maid struggling in the arms of a Greek faun." Whatever it was, it became a magnet for Saint-Gaudens's collection of talented, oddball friends—Maxfield Parrish, Stanford White, and Charles Platt are the names on this list that I recognize. It must be added that my ignorance of the period is impressive, about as close to perfect as ignorance can be.

Ignorance is useful—it lets us look with unassuming, stupid eyes. Everywhere at Aspet, there is evidence of Saint-Gaudens's obsessiveness, his romanticism, his search for gesture. All public statuary is big, but bigness is not the operative quality of his work. It's something else, something in the swirl of the fat pilgrim's coat, something in the muscular arms of his draped women, something in the convincing softness of a marble pillow, made in memory of a bedridden Robert Louis Stevenson. It's wordless and complicated, and reaches a kind of climax in the Adams Memorial, the marker carved for a suicide.

The original is in Rock Creek Cemetery in Washington, but a copy resides here, in one of the high-hedged outdoor rooms that are characteristic of the place. A woman occupies some sort of chair, eyes closed, one hand rising from her lap to touch her hooded face, the entire figure draped in an excess of bed linen that evokes the winding sheet. There is something in her expression that could be joy or could be grief or could be some emotion that can't yet be named. Whatever it is, it's the kind of artifact you can look at for a long time without thinking about anything in particular—your thoughts rotate through a wheel of wonder, peace, and self-immolation. The terrible stillness is so energetic, there is no temptation to even come close to the thing and touch it. It might hurt your hand; it might wake her up; it's better not to.

Aspet calls the visitor from outdoor room to room, where some of Saint-Gaudens's most remarkable work is cloistered. The Robert Gould Shaw Memorial, which stands across the street from the State House on Beacon Hill in Boston, stands here in a slightly different version. The white man on his horse is surrounded by black men on foot, marching toward their doom at Fort Wagner: if you

want all the details, see the movie *Glory*, which will tell
you everything you need to know. What it won't tell you is
how this bas-relief tries hard to free itself from the un-
yielding background plane, how rugged these soldiers
look, how determined in profile. This is a sculpture I grew
up with; it's a place to rendezvous, catty-corner from the
statue of Mary Dyer, across from the Athenaeum, a corner
in Boston where the Brahmins meet.

Birch trees make disorderly allees, and it is fitting
that Aspet has a particularly drunken example—you weave
down the path reciting knock-knock jokes. A broad lawn is
beside you, and an even broader lawn lies ahead, and people romp on them or sun or eat, but after many trips I have
yet to hear a radio. It just isn't a radio kind of place, nor
does it ever seem crowded. Even though there are plenty of
people wandering around, those people are generally
silent. Not with awe, but with contentment and restraint:
Even the dogs some ill-mannered sort has smuggled in
seem sensitive to the aesthetics, carrying their frisbees
with uninsistent dignity, padding along at their owner's
heels. Even the dogs feel it, proof that the enchantment is
real.

Saint-Gaudens suffered horribly toward the end of his
life from cancer, and his search for better health drove
him to build a toboggan run—the scaffolding for this recre-
ational edifice was sixty feet high. You get the feeling he
was the sort of man who liked building it, liked things on

that scale—he also played ice hockey, hiked, and skied. And inspired loyalty: In 1905 his many friends conspired to amuse him with a masque, now infamous, about a golden bowl. From the descriptions it was a good party, with everybody fancied up in chitons like a frat house Friday night, speaking in heroic couplets and hauling the great sculptor around in a chariot, since he was feeling punk. It must have been fun in a mannered way. Later, all the participants were presented with silver medals struck in the shape of the Greek temple they had erected in plaster for the unhinged occasion; later still, Saint-Gaudens built a marble temple on the same spot, and this is where he is buried.

It must have made him grumpy to feel his vitality draining away—he has the face, toward the end of his life, of a scrawny and irritable chicken farmer whose hens have decided not to lay. He looks back at us from behind a sharp beard and craggy eyebrows, pissed off but determined not to complain, still lodged in the apartness that is everywhere at the estate. The story goes, and I believe it, that in August of 1907, a few days before he died, he lay watching the sun go down behind Mount Ascutney. "It's very beautiful," he remarked, "but I want to go *further* away."

Perhaps that's what calls me back to Aspet, past the strip mall and into the New Hampshire countryside. Saint-Gaudens was a man interested in *away*, in the visions that Shaw's men were having off the right-hand edge of the famous panel, visions about what the suicide was dying for. He ranked sunsets a little lower because he looked longer and farther—up on his toes, from the top of his toboggan run, from Aspet past the blue shoulders of the distant hills. But it's curious. He did not sculpt what he saw from this great distance, but instead what it looked like to be looking there.

The grace of these grounds, statues, and gardens is obvious, and if you like your beauty a little mannered and a little overcooked, then that is probably the sort of beauty you will see. But Saint-Gaudens's brand of loveliness also carries a note, not quite of heaven, but of something like heaven that we rightfully yearn to see. Or, if it is heaven, then heaven is more demanding than we imagine, and far more interesting. His statues dismiss the viewer by looking elsewhere, but there is still a transfer of artistic information that the poet Rilke once described as "the start of a terror that we're still able to bear / And the reason we love it so is that it blithely / Disdains to destroy us." This brush against real beauty transcends all the available prettiness at Aspet, and this makes it difficult to take your eyes away.

> **To get there:** Aspet is about twelve miles south of Lebanon, New Hampshire. From I-89, go south on Route 12A through Plainfield toward Cornish; in good time you will see the Blow-Me-Down Mill on your left, and within five hundred feet the entrance to

Aspet appears, also on your left. The house is open for tours during the summer; the modest admission fee can nevertheless be a bummer if you have a large family, and they know this—anyone 17 and under gets in for free. Aspet also offers artist-in-residence programs and holds outdoor concerts every Sunday afternoon during the summer.

Circular Reasoning

Church, School, and Labyrinth

DOWSERS HALL, ABOUT A QUARTER MILE FROM THE
Danville General Store and Vermont Route 2, is
the national headquarters of the American Society of Dowsers. Here you can acquire literature and equipment, sign up for conferences and workshops, and hang
around. Witching for water is a mystery, but there's something wonderfully ordinary about the white cape with its
carpeting and humming computers. The staff is busy but
accommodating and seems to think it is perfectly normal
for people to spend an entire afternoon there doing nothing
much in particular. Dowsers Hall itself, which is attached
to the house, is just that—a large empty room suitable for
wedding receptions—and my vague idea that it might be
full of exhibits proves to be just another vague idea.

I'm here because I learned in the grocery store that an
acquaintance had hired a dowser to locate a well on his
house lot. He drilled where the dowser said to, and the

water was there. There is a lot of water in Vermont, so this outcome didn't particularly surprise me; what did surprise me was the offhandedness of the conversation in the bright, wide aisle, with paper towels in our baskets and violins in the background. "Turns out there's three good wells on the property," he told me.

"The dowser told you that?"

"We picked the one closest to the house," he said, sort of ignoring me.

"Did the dowser pick it?"

"It's a good well—forty gallons a minute. More water than I know what to do with, really."

There was something overconfident and annoying about this transaction, and my unanswered questions have propelled me to Dowsers Hall to stand in front of the racks of literature and re-ask some of my questions. The best way to approach dowsing, I quickly learn, is to take up the rods and try it myself. A sensible, matter-of-fact woman gives me a brief demonstration and then says it is my turn; the metal rods, about the heft and thickness of coat hangers, cross each other obediently as I pass over a water pipe hidden in the floor.

"Whoa," I say. "So this really works, huh?"

"Do you want to try it again?" I'm beginning to see that insisting that people *try* is the dowser's final answer to skepticism. "Try over here." I do. It works. "Now over there."

"Can everybody do this? I mean, this is kind of strange.

What's going on here?"

"Most people can dowse, but it takes practice and skill to be really accurate."

"How does it work?"

She shrugs. "There are a lot of different ideas about it, but nobody really knows. Maybe the explanation has to come later. In the meantime, we judge by results."

I am attracted to the pragmatism of this, and I drift around the office, monkeying with the rods. She watches me patiently but with the air of a person with many other things to do, though I can't think exactly what. The administrative side of dowsing is opaque to me.

"What's that thing over near the parking lot?"

"That's the labyrinth. Would you like to try that, too?"

I STAND IN A LIGHT, steady rain with Lorraine—another ordinary woman who has saved her computer file and taken me outside, where we look at a circular arrangement of stones and mounds and paths, interspersed with a few flowering annuals. It is perfectly round and about thirty-five feet across; I have to ask what relationship this artifact has with dowsing. I somehow picture dowsers as middle-aged men in baseball caps and steel-toed boots, though I'm not entirely sure where this image comes from. "I'm a dowser," says Lorraine. "Dowsing is about asking questions and finding things."

"Did you build this?"

"Well, no. Not really. The path is already there, as part of the earth's energy. We made it, but first we had to discover it."

There are places on the surface of the earth, she says, where labyrinths become manifest. Some of these places are covered by a church, and some of these churches have labyrinths set in the floor, and people walk them. I see what she is getting at: The circular path on the damp ground is a palimpsest, quietly working its way upward, demanding our steps and our attention. It isn't laid on the surface of the earth but teased out of it, sort of like well water. Lorraine talks about ley lines, lines of power, and the need to cleanse the path periodically.

"People come and leave all sorts of things inside it," she explains. "I used to come out with my wand and release all the energy, but not too long ago I asked the labyrinth if it wanted a crystal. It said yes, so I buried one, and it's stayed pretty clean ever since." I have to wonder if this works for bathrooms, too.

True confessions: New Age stuff makes me grumpy and exasperated. My New Age friends tell me it's a flaw in my temperament. I'm out of balance, they say, and resistant, and too quick with the cheap joke. "Your energies are conflicted," a sensitive acquaintance told me once at a barbecue. "And don't eat that hamburger. It makes your aura so *cloudy*." I like hamburger, and I answered this criticism by chewing with my mouth open and wondering aloud why my pyramid doesn't seem to keep my razor blades sharpened so good anymore. It's a wonder I have any friends at all. But I cringe at the trappings and the language of the new religions—angels and crystals and wands and cleansing—and I am secretly cringing now, despite my curiosity, at the start of the path through the labyrinth. I like the contingent, sloppy, cheerful look of the thing, but am embarrassed to go inside.

I try to stall a little. A section of the labyrinth has white sand marking the path; other sections are padded with bark mulch; others are grass. "Does that mean anything?" I ask, pointing to the mosaic effect of the different colors.

"Let's walk it together," Lorraine says. "It's easier to do it than to try to explain."

"If I do this wrong," I ask, hoping for a long, philosophical answer, "will it be mad at me?"

"Nope," she says. "You can't hurt it, and it can't hurt you." And, in what I am coming to think of as dowserspeak, she adds, "Just *try* it."

We begin the circular walk, and she asks me to let go of interfering thought forms, find my balance, awaken my compassion, and be open to divine guidance.

"Can you feel your chakras spinning?" she asks.

"Do I want them to spin?"

She laughs at my alarm, and explains that it's not important to feel them. It is the path that matters, and finding the right speed along the path, and using the path as a centering tool. "It's better to walk it without shoes on," she says as we approach the center, "but it's wet out here today."

And she's right, it is. At the heart of the labyrinth we pause and look around us, enjoying the cool air and the tap of water in a stand of nearby trees.

ABOUT A WEEK LATER I find myself admiring the curved surfaces of the only round schoolhouse in America, which sits about four feet from the paved road in Brookline, across from the town offices. It's brick, and for a structure built a long time ago on a decidedly perfunctory foundation, it's in wonderful condition—smooth and confident and penetrated by big windows. If you stop the car, you can peer in these windows and see a serene and intelligent room with modest but sweeping dimensions, anchored by a woodstove squatting in the middle.

It's a small school by our standards—maybe twenty or so feet in diameter—and there's no resource room, drinking fountain, or flush toilets. Still, it has the indefinable air of *school*. It's a round school, though—perfectly round—with a little brick wart on one side for an entryway, and if it happens to be Monday, you can go across the road and ask the town clerk to let you in. Then you can experience the roundness from the inside and consider the misdeeds and the possible redemption of John Wilson.

Wilson showed up in Brookline about 1820, where

he designed the school and taught for about a year. He then moved on to teach and practice medicine in and around Dummerston, Newfane, and, after 1835, Brattleboro. By all accounts he was sophisticated, well educated, flirtatious, and a little bit peculiar. He always wore a silk scarf around his neck, even on the hottest days, and when he died in 1847 it became clear why: He was covering up a nasty scar that looked like an old rope burn. His left leg had a bullet wound of about the same vintage and a part of his heel was shot away—a little digging and checking revealed that Dr. John Wilson was, in truth, the notorious and charming robber, Captain Thunderbolt.

Captain Thunderbolt—with a name like that it's hard not to think of leotards, capes, masks, and men who wear their underpants outside their clothes, but this reaction is bred of Saturday-morning television, which of course came later. Captain Thunderbolt was a highwayman in England (I almost wrote "English highwayman," but that, strictly speaking, is untrue, since he was born in Scotland). He got his name from the speed, daring, and precision of his holdups; he would appear out of nowhere with his accomplice, Captain Lightfoot. These two robbers stopped coaches, kissed women in a courtly way, and relieved men of their pocketbooks. If all this sounds like a bodice ripper with a credibility problem, it is not my fault. Why bother with fiction when the truth will do?

John Wilson was good-looking, suave, and something

of a drinker. Women liked him, and after he went into hiding across the sea in Vermont, there is oblique evidence that he kept on kissing hands even after he married a woman from Brattleboro. This woman later divorced him, and her grounds were probably abundant and may have included certain suspicions about his past. In 1847, when he lay on his deathbed still wearing his scarf and shoes, he asked to be buried dressed just as he was. The doctor and his friends apparently agreed to this but forgot to take into account the meddlesome habits of undertakers, who like to wash and embalm the recently departed. His scarred body and his dashing past were exposed at the exact moment when he was beyond caring, leaving us with a memorable corpse and a swell story.

And, of course, this unusual building. Nothing in the Captain Thunderbolt narrative really explains the Brookline schoolhouse. Supposedly, the size and the placement of these graceful windows allowed him to see if anyone was coming to arrest him, but accounting for the serenity of this building presents a separate problem. It calls to mind the other round thing behind Dowsers Hall, and I have to pause: Did Captain Thunderbolt really design it, or did it work its way to the surface and ask to be designed? I notice again that the curving brick walls have shifted very little since 1821, as if the structure is blessed with extra cohesiveness.

I MAY BE IN THE GRIP of a mild mania because a few days after visiting the schoolhouse in Brookline, I find myself peering into the windows of yet another arresting circular structure, the Round Church in Richmond. This eyeful of a building was constructed in 1813, making it eight years older than the much smaller building a hundred miles away. Strictly speaking, the Round Church isn't round; it has sixteen sides, making it a sedecagon, or at least I think it does. Whatever it's called the effect is circular—the eye smooths the corners into curves.

Local lore is that seventeen housewrights agreed to work on the meetinghouse, one for each side and the last one for the cupola. As a practical matter they probably worked on all the sides all together, starting from the ground up, but there's an idea here about shared responsibility shared precisely, with explicit boundaries. This idea carried over into the use of the structure since five different denominations used the building at the same time, with slots reserved for Catholics, Methodists, Unitarians, Baptists, and Congregationalists. This led, almost inevitably, to quarreling: Some of the worst squabbles in history have been triggered by exactly this kind of sectarian propinquity. As time went by and money became available, the different groups built churches of their own, and it may be an oddity of its history that right now nobody worships there at all.

The building was designed and the construction supervised by William Rhodes. He was a native of Warwick,

Rhode Island, and came to Vermont by way of Claremont, New Hampshire, a town that built a round church of its own in 1806. Rhodes already lived in Richmond by then but probably went back to Claremont to see his relatives, and he must have taken a professional interest in what the good people of New Hampshire were up to with their round architecture. Thus we can trace the probable source of the design of this peculiar building. But Rhodes, unlike Dr. John Wilson, seems to have led an exemplary and uninteresting life. He bought and sold land, registered a livestock mark, and served as a town officer in Richmond. He did not hold up coaches, and he did not kiss hands. The two men, however, are linked by an architectural impulse and by their willingness to build on a circular plan.

The building is open daily in the summertime, which the people of Richmond construct to be from Independence Day through the end of the foliage season. You can stand in the middle and feel a kind of lift—a high, circular gallery forms the second floor, the ceiling soars, and the sun pours in (when it isn't raining) in an unusually evocative way. It's hard not to feel that you stand at the center of some sort of creation—the Round Church has the simple and aggressive beauty of those Renaissance drawings of the Copernican universe, ringed and musical and comforting. Constructing a round building is a real pain but worth it—you do achieve this slight, dizzying spin and a hint of the world's unity.

I TEST-DRIVE my new dowsing rods in the yard, looking for water. I am foggy whether there is likely to be groundwater on my quarter-acre village lot—we are served by the town water system, and as a result I have never given the presence or absence of other water even a moment's thought. My teenage son watches a little warily as I wander around the place; each time I cross an invisible line between the house and the honeysuckle, the rods form a precise X, and then uncross as I get farther away. It's a queer phenomenon; I ask Nick to try. Although the reaction is not as distinct, it is still manifest—each time he crosses the same line, the rods respond. I'm not sure, but this might be the town's service line. *Not that kind of water*, I tell the rods— I have learned that it is important to address dowsing rods sort of the way you address an intelligent dog, though without saying anything out loud. The church across the street has erected a large striped tent and is having some sort of yard sale. There are perhaps a dozen people poking through the kitchen curtains, hand drills, and salt-and-pepper shakers. As I criss-cross the yard I notice how they fall silent as I come toward them, then chatter with relief as I turn away.

Show me something missing, something lost, I tell my divining rods. The question feels a little too open-ended, but I figure if I'm going to look silly, I might as well get something out of the humiliation. I sweep back and forth, enjoying the press of sun first on my neck, then on my face,

and the dowsing rods respond almost wildly as I approach
the shaggy stand of lilac appropriately called the Jungle.
Something lost? Something in here? The rods are confident, almost emphatic; I reach between the suckers and retrieve a greenish tennis ball.

THAT'S PRETTY GOOD, I decide, although it isn't my tennis
ball. I have never owned one—I don't have a racket and
don't have a puppy, and what else is there that can be done
with one? I roll it between my palms and admire its brisk
fuzziness, its slight crinkliness even after a year in the lilac
wilderness. Also, I notice with pleasure, it's spherical, and
I'm developing an affinity for discovering curved things. I'm
impressed enough to think about going back to Danville—
I'm interested in closure, symmetry, and I like the Northeast Kingdom. I've been known to drive to the Kingdom on
the flimsiest excuses because I like the scenery, the high
vistas, and the abundance of grasshoppers.

I also like food, and I find myself eating a large and
gummy lunch in St. Johnsbury, close by Danville, and
thinking about Captain Thunderbolt and William Rhodes
and Lorraine. There is some underlying and agreeable
sameness about all these circles, and I realize to my surprise that I have come to the Kingdom to walk the labyrinth
again. This time I want to walk it alone and in my own way;
I wonder whether putting gravy on my french fries will to-
tally mess up my aura. I put the gravy on anyway but in a

circle, with a few inner loops for my chakras, whatever those are. Thus cleansed and fortified, I go back to Dowsers Hall and remove my shoes.

Nothing interesting happens—my feet get cold, and a territorial, unseen bird beeps at me from the bushes—but there is something unified and pleasant about the exercise, on a par with folding clean laundry that has dried in the sun. As I walk, I wonder a little about the idea of circles pushing through the earth to demand a schoolhouse here, a church there, and a maze somewhere else; it reminds me of something the writer Michael Dorris once said about how fictional characters present themselves: "We dream about them, you know, and draw their pictures." This oblique metaphor works for me, and explains the rounds I have been making and my satisfaction when I arrive, in due course, at the center. The fingerprint whorls of the labyrinth rotate around me—this gentle, familiar dizziness seems to be what happens at the center of all round things. I think the dowsers are right, that people should just *try* this and that it does no harm. A journey, after all, is more than the fact of arrival.

To get there: The Brookline schoolhouse is off Route 30 where it runs through Newfane. Turn east where the flea market is held (one of the largest in Vermont, held Sundays from May to October), and follow Grassy Brook Road for about five miles. The schoolhouse is on your left. If it's Monday, and if you ask nicely, the town clerk will let you in; there is no admission.

The Round Church in Richmond is off Route 2; when you get to the village, turn south at the traffic lights, and go over the iron bridge. The church is set back behind a modest green on your left. The church is open weekends from Memorial Day to July 4, and daily from July 4 through foliage season. The hours are 10 to 4, and there is no admission.

Dowsers Hall is also off Route 2, but is a long way east of Richmond in Danville. At the general store, turn south and follow the signs—the hall is on your right. The labyrinth is tucked in behind the hall, just southeast of the parking lot. The headquarters of the American Society of Dowsers is open on weekdays; people are welcome to walk the labyrinth at their convenience.

One of Vermont's most widely admired round structures is the Round Barn at the Shelburne Museum on Route 7 south of Burlington. It is beautifully preserved, and it is big, and there is a hefty admission fee.

Border Lands

The Irish Invasion of Canada

NORTH AND EAST OF BURLINGTON THE TOPOGRAPHY
changes, and the big furry mountains give way to
open, rolling hills. By Vermont standards it's
flat—long vistas appear, and the sky lowers, and you can
see silos glinting on the horizon, black cattle receding, and
blue rain falling ten miles away. Instead of high wooded
hills and deep river valleys there are gentle undulations, as
if we were suddenly set out to sea. Trees are fewer and
seem taller, and they gather in clumps and copses and
wear European expressions.

These are the border lands, where Vermont touches
the prosperous farmland of southern Quebec. Jay Peak
with its ski area dominates the eastern horizon, but skiers
and tourists don't seem to wander much into this quiet,
tended valley; even the most admirable and comprehen-
sive guide to Vermont completely ignores the existence of
Franklin, Berkshire, Sheldon, and Highgate. Which is odd,

I think. This land is groomed and gorgeous, and it has the distinction of being the staging ground for the Irish invasion of Canada. This incident, too, is largely ignored, and disappears into the same silence.

The Fenian Raids of 1866 and 1870 probably look like monkey business to most twentieth-century eyes. Irish American soldiers, trained in and tempered by the Civil War, converged on the area, bringing with them the unusual idea of crossing over and establishing a free Irish republic in Canada. It's a startling agenda. Isn't Canada our friend, our trade partner, our gigantic ally to the north? Today it would take an unhinged American to lift arms against so large and benevolent a neighbor, and you would think any adjacent American with good sense would take away the gun, administer a scolding, and invite the insurgent back to the home place to discuss the matter over a hot dinner. It was crazy, but it was also serious, dangerous, exciting, and morally ambiguous. This may explain why the Fenian Raids are not taught in our schools and do not transmit as part of our national folklore. The attitude is quite different across the border in Quebec.

The Fenians derived their name from the legendary Irish warriors of the second and third centuries, and their rise in America during the nineteenth century was supposed to be a secret, but not a particularly well-kept one. As things heated up along the border, the *Burlington Free Press* of May 24, 1870, reported that "all is rumor and uncertainty," but the muddle was over what the Fenians were up to; their existence was common knowledge. Messages coming in from St. Albans, Port Henry, Albany, Rutland, Boston, Hartford, Providence, and New York City indicated that thousands of Fenians—anywhere from four thousand to twenty thousand, depending on which rumors you decide are credible—were on the move. "The Vermont Central [Railway] managers recorded dispatches from Boston yesterday inquiring on what terms they would carry a *thousand men* from Boston over their road today and have also, as we hear, been notified to provide cars for an unusual number of passengers tonight," says the paper. The excitable italics are theirs. The *Free Press* goes on to observe that this massing of Irish patriots is different from the Fenian skirmish of 1866 at Fort Erie in that: "Now the Fenians keep their own counsel as far as possible, and that this time their arms are on the border before them." These arms, according to the rumors, were also substantial: twenty cannon, uncounted loads of swords and rifles, and a hundred and twenty-five teams loaded with provisions and supplies. Between Burlington and St. Albans, people flocked to the rail stations to watch the trains go by. "Quite large crowds had collected and there was a liberal amount of encouragement in the way of waving hats, etc., by the sympathizers."

This sympathy for the Fenian cause was complicated. It was true that Americans were mad at the Canadians at the end of the Civil War, and Vermonters were particularly mad—the northernmost act of aggression of the Civil War could be laid at the feet of Canada. In October of 1864 a band of Confederate soldiers had slipped across the border and ridden to St. Albans, where they robbed the banks, set fire to houses, shot up the town, and skittered back to safety. A band of citizens chased after them and recovered some of the cash but not, as the cop shows say, the perps— and there was outrage that the Canadians would permit a raid to originate from its territory into ours.

This raid was one of a string of annoyances. British Canada was also where the Confederate warships *Alabama* and *Florida* were constructed, and these vessels inflicted considerable damage to Union shipping. As early as 1861 the *New York Herald* was bristling about Canadian efforts to undermine the North, pointing out that, once the Civil War ended (which lots of people thought would happen quickly), "[f]our hundred thousand thoroughly disciplined troops will ask no better occupation than to destroy the last vestige of British rule on the American continent, and annex Canada to the United States." The *Trent* Affair in November of 1861 was another irritant and put the Americans in a bad light: The freedom of the open seas was violated when the warship *San Jacinto* took two former US senators, by then Confederate commissioners, off a British mail packet near Bermuda. It was a precarious time, and feelings were running high; in April, the opening salvos of the

Civil War boomed over Fort Sumter.

Still, most people were simply too pooched after the Civil War to contemplate a serious quarrel with Canada. What's more, the Fenian movement, despite being fought almost entirely by veterans of the Civil War, was not really an American movement. It was an Irish one—it was about the Protestant Ascendancy, the Potato Famine, the evictions of the 1840s, and the trauma of the Irish diaspora. I'm not sure it's possible to overstate the central tragedies of Irish history in the mid-nineteenth century, which began with starvation and sickness, phase-shifted through indifference, and ended by carrying millions into emigration and exile. Many of those exiles ended up here, in New England, where Irish nationalism seemed to thrive. The Fenian Brotherhood is said to have raised a following of fifty thousand Irish Americans during this time, and their goal was to return to Ireland, evict the British, and establish full autonomy to a depleted and unhappy land.

How this goal got deflected into the idea of invading Canada is a little less clear, though it seems to have happened during a summit of Fenians in Philadelphia in 1865. Canada was under British rule and was, after all, quite a lot closer than Dublin, though the logic, both then and now, seems a little oblique. "What the Fenians expect to accomplish of real service to their cause," said the *Free Press* on the eve of battle, "is difficult to see. The Dominion is indeed a British province, but it is one that is of no service to

England, and the English government has avowed its willingness to relinquish all care of it. If it were a supposable case that the Fenians could take Canada, the question arises, how can it possibly affect the independence or welfare of Ireland?" This is a good question. That the raids might lead to war between the US and Canada didn't seem to trouble the well-wishers as they waved from the rail platforms. Action is its own kind of answer, and for the moment it was action that mattered.

ON WEDNESDAY MORNING, May 26, 1870, the *Free Press* reported that about five hundred Fenians had marched to Hubbard's Corner, about half a mile beyond the village of Franklin and about a mile from the Canadian border. This number would later be revised downward to two hundred—the Fenian general, John O'Neill, had called for an army and gotten arms, but no men to speak of. When he met the Boston train at St. Albans, he expected a thousand men from Massachusetts; fewer than fifty appeared. In light of this shortage, O'Neill decided to abandon a rather ambitious plan of capturing the rail lines that led from Montreal to the border and instead to focus his efforts at Pigeon Hill, across the border from Franklin. But even this plan was weakened by the absence of soldiers. His many boxes of rifles were useless without people to carry them, and they lay open by the roadsides, their contents spilling over in the thin spring sunshine.

George Foster, the US marshal for Vermont, turned up in the Fenian camp. He wanted to read President Grant's neutrality proclamation to the soldiers, which was an overt warning against breaching the peace between the US and Canada, and against "aiding, countenancing, abetting, or taking part" in unlawful proceedings like this one. He did read Grant's message—to little effect—and at the same time probably got a close look at the numbers and the situation. As he orated, the Fenians huddled around O'Neill, worried that Foster would arrest him. Which Foster might have been tempted to do since O'Neill had broken the neutrality laws before, when he led the 1866 raid on Fort Erie where four Canadians were killed and about fifty wounded. For various good reasons, Foster abstained. Whether O'Neill was a patriot or simply a hothead depended on your point of view, but Foster's position was delicate and complicated. O'Neill was both an Irish freedom fighter and an American citizen, with the free passage and assembly rights of all other American citizens. O'Neill could plan an invasion, scatter guns about, speak sedition, and march on the border, but until he crossed it there was not much Foster or anyone else could do.

Foster was in for a busy day: As the soldiers moved north from Franklin village, the US marshal appeared in their midst again. He had been over on the Canadian side and now told the Fenians that Pigeon Hill—which the Canadians called Eccles Hill—was already defended, and they would be fired on as soon as they crossed the next rise. As with the proclamation, the Fenians listened, but again did not pay the right kind of attention—they used this intelligence as the cue to begin loading their weapons and shedding their overcoats. Foster also pointed out to O'Neill that the Fenians were blocking the road, preventing the passage of citizens. This, he said, "would not do." The guard across the road was withdrawn, allowing a band of newspaper reporters through in advance of the line; a slight tinge of slapstick was already beginning to color the proceedings.

O'NEILL WAS STILL HOPING that a large contingent of New York Fenians would appear, which may explain his strange mixture of courage and dithering. He assembled his men. "This is the advance guard of the Irish American Army," he told them, "for the liberation of Ireland from the yoke of the oppressor. For your own country you now enter that of the enemy. The eyes of your countrymen are upon you." To which William Cronan of Burlington replied, lifting his hat, "General, I am proud that Vermont has the honor of leading this advance. Ireland may depend on us to do our duty." This is odd rhetoric, in which the idea of "country" seems to slide like overcooked okra around the plate, but that is the heart of the Fenian story and perhaps its point, so nobody noticed. A line of men formed across the road near the brick farmhouse of Alvah Richards, and a company went ahead of this line to cross the wooden bridge over a modest stream called the Pike River. As Foster had warned, the Canadians opened fire—one Fenian was killed immediately and another wounded. Another was killed and two more were wounded as the invaders hastened for cover in the woods, and some of the newspaper reporters mentioned earlier suddenly found themselves caught between the lines. Exposed to the crossfire and with nothing but notebooks and pencils to show for themselves, they scurried to the farmhouse and took shelter. The Fenians returned fire rather wildly into the rocks and trees, and, because they were retreating anyway, O'Neill told his men to fall back out of range.

This is where Marshal George Foster turned up again. Foster and his deputy, Thomas Failey, had been patiently following events from a prudent distance. After the first encounter and regrouping, they saw O'Neill wander away from the Fenian line, reportedly looking for the New York reinforcements. He didn't find them and encountered only a badly wounded Irish American soldier. As the general paused to talk to him, Foster appeared at his elbow: "I arrest you in the name of the United States government," he said, perhaps rather congenially, for it is clear that Foster was a man of remarkably good temper. One account even has the two men shaking hands. "No," said O'Neill. "You must not. I will not be arrested." But he was—Failey materialized with a carriage, and O'Neill was stuffed inside, and they drove swiftly back through the Fenian rear guard, through the New York reinforcements that had just arrived and through the rolling landscape toward Burlington. Foster told O'Neill to be quiet and not to call to his soldiers for help or intervention, at the risk of his life, and O'Neill didn't. If there is a hero in this mess, it may be George Foster, who emerges as a man of persistence, diplomacy, decisiveness, and controlled ferocity.

THE BATTLE OF ECCLES HILL, as the Canadians call it, was fought in what is now a parklike valley between the still-standing brick farmhouse and the rocky prominence that gave the Canadian militia such a decisive upper hand. What the Fenians didn't know—and perhaps it's just as well—is that only forty men occupied the Canadian position. More defenders showed up after O'Neill was arrested, and in the lingering light of a spring evening the Canadians advanced, flushed a few Fenian stragglers, and toyed with the idea of crossing the border to speed the retreat, make a little merry, and put a finishing flourish on a gratifying victory. Their leaders talked them out of this—it would only annoy the American authorities, who had been helpful, plus it was getting dark. Time for supper.

There is an innocence to this old battleground. Like most places where decisive things happened, the echo of the past is half-absorbed by the vegetation of the present. This is true of Concord, of Bunker Hill, even of Gettysburg with its rows of stones. A smallish stream runs through this valley, and an unused road; the wooden bridge the Fenians crossed has been replaced by a causeway and an impressive metal culvert. You are not supposed to cross the border here, and signs in both French and English direct you to the customs stations, one in either direction, several miles away. You can linger, though, on this old right-of-way and see where the bullets flew. On the Canadian side, at the summit of the hill, you can see where most of them flew from, and you can admire a tall marker and a small cannon, perhaps the same cannon the Canadians took from the Fenians during the retreat, and the only major weapon deployed during the argument. The Fenians fired it once and missed; they were too busy with other things to fire it again.

The peacefulness of the site—the scattered houses, the fragrant farmland, the gurgling stream—only seems to emphasize that this was a place where things could have gone quite differently. This is another characteristic of battlegrounds, and they attract us as pivot points, or perhaps doorways into some parallel universe. It was the Fenian posture toward Canada that speeded up the process of confederation among the provinces north of the border; it was the defeat of the Fenians at Eccles Hill (or Pigeon Hill, depending on where you are standing and whose story you are reading) that eventually led to a refocusing of that movement and the rise of Sinn Fein. There is a doubling not just of names but of possibilities. Had the Fenian movement lived up to its advance billing, even by half, they probably would have carried the day. What do we make of an Irish enclave north of Franklin? Would it preclude or cancel the 1916 Easter Rising along the Liffey, or the linguistic factionalism of the Quebecois?

One of the strange joys of the border lands is that within moments of crossing over, nobody understands a word you say. This is overstatement—most Quebecois are courteously bilingual—but an overstatement that fits. There is an air of doubleness in this corner of the world— the country rolls and swells identically on both sides of the boundary, and beef cattle chew on the same varieties of silage wearing the same placid expression, yet French Canada remembers the Fenian Raids and, for the most part, Americans don't. I can't decide if this annoys or saddens me, but I can observe the palimpsest of history in this unspoiled place.

IN ALL FAIRNESS I did find a marker on the Vermont side, but I have to add that it seems to be deliberately placed so that no one can really read it. It sits about twelve miles from the battleground, where Route 105 in Sheldon Junction whizzes over the broad back of the Mississquoi River. You can't pull over next to it, and if you do turn around, find your way back, and park your car on the east end of the bridge, you get to pick your way along a nonexistent

shoulder, caught between a metal railing and the *whoosh* of
cars and semis. FENIAN RAIDS, the sign says, ATTEMPTED
CANADIAN INVASION NORTH OF HERE, 1866 AND 1870. The
sign was placed by the Vermont Division of Historic
Preservation, which has scattered a hundred or more
equivalent signs around the state, pointing to things as diverse and distracting as first ski tows, first canals, final
resting places, and the invention of the platform scale.

"After the Civil War," says the sign's narrative text,
"two attempts of Irish patriots to invade Canada and set
up a free Irish republic were repulsed between Franklin
and Cook's Corners. Fenians gathered in St. Albans,
marched via Sheldon to the border, but were stopped by
Canadian arms and U.S. authorities." Which is true as far
as it goes, but the sign, for me, sparks only anxiety. As I
decipher it, clinging to the cold metal and concrete of the
bridge, an irritated motorist honks at me: *Get off the effing
bridge!*

I'm not criticizing, or at least I'm not trying to criticize
(there's a difference), but the placement of this sign does
point to the general placement of these events in the American imagination. As an experiment, I e-mailed and called
around to about a dozen educated, alert friends, most of
them Vermonters. "Don't look it up and don't ask your
neighbor," I said, "but just tell me truthfully. Do you know
about the Fenian Raids?" I got some wonderful guesses,
and some of those guesses included passing references to

the Irish, but none of these people with advanced degrees had even a vague clue of what had come about within an easy drive of where they were sitting.

It's not possible for everyone to know everything, and it would be boring if they did, but this blanket of not knowing is, in itself, a kind of information. The day I visited the battlefield, wending my way from the Canadian side, sizable packs of Quebecois teenagers were also descending on the monument, the cannon, and the quiet valley—the marker and its story were part of a school project on tourism and local history. As they swarmed merrily, making notes and giggling, two women emerged from the house directly adjacent to the site with the idea of getting out of their own driveway. "Lots of people come here," one of the women tells me in the pure and inimitable accent of northern Vermont. "I've lived here all my life, and I've seen plenty of people come to visit." She mourns with us the passing of the original wooden bridge, swept away in the floods of 1998, and we learn that the battleground is not a public park but her personal property. Replacing the bridge with a causeway cost her a pretty penny; keeping the place groomed and mowed can't be cheap, either. I ask: Do you mind all the people? "No. They like to come. And we have to mow it because my daughter, she has the allergies." Her unaccented English, her matter-of-factness, and her tolerance seem to concatenate with the marker, the cannon, and the whole Fenian-Canadian story. Something happened here, and it was something Americans are the poorer for ignoring.

THE PLAYWRIGHT EUGENE O'NEILL once announced: "Nothing says more about me than the fact that I am Irish." And it's at least partly true—that he was born in New York and attended Princeton and Harvard seem like accidents of social history. What matters is O'Neill's obsessive, disenfranchised, yearning Celtic soul; he earned his Nobel Prize the hard way, with labor and self doubt. My own soul is only partly Celtic and only partly prone to yearning—like many white Americans I have abandoned ethnic ties in exchange for the generic pleasures and pains of citizenship. Until recently, I always had an idea—albeit a vague one—that this was a good thing: I can buddy up with Jews, Lebanese, Poles, and Germans, and we can all go for pizza without armed conflict.

But this blending was also won the hard way. In 1861, Patrick Dunny wrote home to his family in Carlow about the Battle of Bull Run, and in his letter he describes yet another kind of doubling:

> Two Irish regiments met on that dreadful
> battlefield. One was the 69th of New York, a nobler
> set of men was not in the world, who carried the
> green flag of Erin all day proudly through the
> shower of bullets. The other Irish regiment was

from Louisiana, also composed of good Irishmen who think just as much of Ireland. They opposed the 69th all day, trying to capture the poor green flag, and they took it up four times but four times had to give it up.

There were more lives lost over that flag than any one object on the field. The fourth time it was taken by the rebels, the poor 69th was so worn out that they were not able to take it back. But a man, a sergeant in the nearly all-Irish 79th regiment, cried out that the flag of his country was going with the rebels. He leveled his rifle and shot the bearer of it dead, and then he and his company made a bayonet charge and rescued the flag and bore it back in triumph to the 69th.

This is a moving and rather exasperating piece of storytelling, and of a piece with the Fenian Raids. That the opening battle of the Civil War was shaped, at least in part, by misdirected Irish passions is something we should know—it teaches us something important about the complex and deceptive arrows of history.

BACK IN THE BORDER LANDS, I find myself taking pictures, first from one side of the valley, shooting across into Canada, and then from the other, shooting into the United States. I know these pictures will be uninteresting, but I take them anyway because the idea of them interests me. Boundaries interest me. At the time of the raids, boundaries may have had a more provisional quality—this was a time when states could secede, the nation could move westward, and Fenians could think seriously about capturing a part of Canada. At one time both Vermont and Texas were independent republics; those lines were eventually softened into statehood, and some people still regret it, but this is not my point. My point, to some degree, is the foreknowledge that the pictures will be uninteresting— the narrative is there, in the landscape, but a picture will not tell the story. It will not show the boundary. Each time I look at the pictures I will have to reconstruct it, to remind myself that it is there.

The small corner of me that is Irish—from Tyrone, home of the great family of O'Neills, home of spinners of smooth linen—yearns in a decidedly Celtic way for more glory, more closure, and more reassurance than this pretty valley can offer. I won't get it: the Irish story is still unfolding under our noses, but I can still take my pictures and insist that what happened here was important. They were poorly planned, pushy, off-target, and unrealistic, but the Fenian Raids should never be forgotten.

To get there: There is no access to the battleground from the Vermont side of the border, but you reach it via Eccles Hill Road in Quebec. Cross the border on Route 235 at Morse's Line and follow this road about five miles to the first crossroads. Turn right; Eccles Hill Road is another ten or twelve miles on the right, and the monument will soon appear, also on your right. The battleground is at the end of the road. The brick farmhouse that served as a sort of paperweight for the action is within fifty feet of the border on the American side. We were told there are bullet holes in the house, inflicted during the raid, and this seems probable, but it is a private home, still owned by the Richards family. Visitors should respect that privacy.

Notes and Selected Readings

I HAD AN INSANELY GOOD TIME writing this book, and at least half the fun of it was the general and background reading I was allowed to do. The oddest things came in handy, and the idea behind this section of the book is not to be scholarly or responsible, but to share some of the titles that inspired and instructed me as I wandered from place to place. The following list is by no means exhaustive; worse, some of the selections point to material I never used directly, but relied on for insight and background color. These books framed my approach and were invaluable in the shaping of my ideas.

General information: The guide to Vermont that I relied on most was Christina Tree and Peter S. Jennison's *Vermont: An Explorer's Guide*. It is engaging and well organized and contains lots of useful information about each region of the state. It also has information for people who need a place to sleep and do not pack a lunch—I am not a member of this tribe, but others are. More interesting is the National

Survey's *Gazetteer of Vermont Heritage*, published in 1976 and still in print because it is too entertaining not to be: It contains a general history of the state, profiles of each town, biographical sketches of Vermonters too fractious to be forgotten, and plenty of old line cuts and photographs. Another general reference work on Vermont is Esther Swift's *Vermont Place-Names: Footprints of History.* After a long, sad period out of print, this book has been revived and is now generally available again. This rather weighty tome captures the bounce of the Vermont temperament by looking closely at the almost reckless abundance of its place names. Even though I didn't use any of the material in it, *Vermont Place-Names* is close to being required reading for anyone who cares about the history of the state.

For maps, turn to Northern Cartographic, which publishes a detailed gazetteer in book form, or to the official folding map of the Vermont Travel Division. I am inordinately fond of this second item, not just because it is meticulous, but because it has the magic words "for free distribution" printed on the front.

Taken for Granite: For background information about the Vermont granite industry, you might want to read Rod Clarke's *Carved in Stone*, available through the Rock of Ages Corporation. This modest paperback covers the economic and social reverberations of the industry and is full of engaging photographs. There are other histories of the granite industry, but this was the most inviting I found; the editorial emphasis falls on the lives of the quarrymen and the development of Barre as a distinctive place. My information on the Corti incident in 1903 is extracted mostly from contemporary newspaper accounts, and the flavor of the piece is derived directly from the stones in Hope Cemetery.

Justin Morgan Had a Life: While looking for background on the life of Justin Morgan the man, I had particular fun with Betty Bandel's *Sing the Lord's Song in a Strange Land: The Life of Justin Morgan.* Information on Justin Morgan the horse can be had from the American Morgan Horse Association, among other places. Lippitt Morgans have their own breeding register and sometimes hold Lippitt-only competitions—these are the old-style Morgans closer to Figure's original type. I have to confess a prejudice against some of the training and showing practices used on what are called gaited horses, and many Morgans are shown as gaited horses, but to see these performances is to miss much of what the horse is capable of. Morgans are generally natural and free in their movement, despite being a little short strided, and do not usually display the jittery, false, and pointless flourishes associated with this kind of riding. That they can do it only reinforces my point; they can also cut cattle and win the egg-and-spoon race at the local gymkhana.

Facing West: Information on the Mormon movement is generally available through a variety of sources, almost all of which have an ax to grind one way or another. The topic seems to inspire a level of shrillness completely out of keeping with the daily realities of Mormon culture today, and the greatest and grumpiest noises arise from ex-Mormons. Fawn Brodie's *No Man Knows My History* is a temperate and restrained biography of Joseph Smith, but it still triggered a lot of yelling; the general reader may want to stay clear of that particular fray. As literature, *The Book of Mormon* is rather deep footing, but as a seminal document it is worth the labor; the westward movement of the Saints is part of our national narrative and is recounted in general histories of the period.

Urban Glaciation: In this chapter I reference Charles Johnson's *The Nature of Vermont*; I also made good use of Peter Jennison's *The Roadside History of Vermont*. The geology of the region is complicated, and to get a grip on how Vermont relates to the larger formation of New England, I used Chad and Maureen Raymo's *Written in Stone*. This is a good book for readers with no specific background in geology, but I must add that some of the maps are alarming—in one, Montpelier has migrated to Jeffersonville.

Indian Stones: The captivity narrative of Susanna Johnson can be found, as I mention in the essay, in Colin Calloway's *North Country Captives*. This same author has written other books, notably *Dawnland Encounters*, about the relations between settlers and Native Americans, and the April 1951 newsletter of the Vermont Historical Society offers up a picture of the two Indian Stones from before the time they were re-erected in a granite protective casing. For an amusing and puzzling look at what can happen to a local image over time, turn to page 18 of the National Survey's *Gazetteer of Vermont Heritage*. There are the Indian Stones, but with the human figure on the larger stone transformed into a devil and the inscription overwritten by the single word *temperance*. I find this appropriation arresting and enchanting. Its interest is only increased because nobody seems to know how it happened.

Fireworks: Much of the information about the Randolph fires is firsthand since I stood on the sidewalk and watched them unfold; back issues of the *Herald of Randolph* were also called upon. I think this essay is probably the first general account of all three fires, and a better history could almost certainly be compiled by Jeff Staudinger, who directed the nonprofit that worked tirelessly to restore the downtown, or by members of that nonprofit's board. My only excuse is that none of these fine people have the leisure that I have had. This account is a personal perspective only.

Tales from the Cryptozoologists: Narratives of the sightings of the Lake Champlain monster, Champ, appeared in *Cryptozoology* in 1982 and 1990, authored by Joseph Zarzynski, and a compilation of sighting reports also appears on the Champ Quest Web site (http://homepages.together.net/~ultisrch/) referenced in the essay. There is an abundance of general background information on water monsters—so much that a general reader hardly knows where to begin. Kendrick Frazier has written at least two books that address the intersection of science and the paranormal, and the mathematician and puzzlemeister Martin Gardner has written at length on much the same thing. *No Mercy*, by Redmond O'Hanlon, is only obliquely about the Mokele-mbembe, but it is a rich and remarkable book that lots of people ought to read, and tends to confirm my own belief about the emotional logic embedded in these animals and how this logic points to their origins.

Wheat Paste and Rags: The Bread and Puppet Museum sells a range of pamphlets and books, most of them wonderful but puzzling. The *Subversive Museum* booklet referenced in the story was acquired there, and there are probably other collections of photographs and essays that an inquisitive mind would enjoy. As this book goes to press, the assault in the campground is being gnashed through the legal system. The shows go on, often at community festivals around the state, though the scale of these events is modest. The loss of the scope and momentum of the Circus can't really be measured yet, but there are other outdoor rituals, such as the Burning Man in Nevada, that are available for those of us who need this kind of communal ritual in our lives.

A Very '70s Thing to Do: Background materials on the art on Vermont's interstate are skimpy—the Vermont Historical Society (VHS) library in Montpelier has a copy of the symposium publication I referred to in the essay; there is also an engaging but unbound general inventory of Vermont statuary, compiled by Vermont SOS, that the librarian lugs to your table in a big cardboard box. I found this very entertaining—the abundance and sporadic nuttiness of outdoor sculpture around the state is impressive—and the VHS library is a grand place to while away an afternoon. Symposiums (that ought to be symposia, but I can't bring myself to use this snooty construction) continue to crop up around the state, and the Champ sculpture in marble referenced in "Tales from the Crypto-zoologists" is an outcome of one of these gatherings. There, along the Burlington bike path, are sculptures of canoes, rollerblades, Neptune, Pegasus, and simple waves like fossils from the floor of some great inland sea. If I got the story right, these works were carved into the waste marble that was used, along with other stones, to build the jetty and shoreline along this section of the lake. Marble is found in Vermont around Proctor and Danby.

The Demands of Heaven: The life of Augustus Saint-Gaudens is discussed in Louise Tharp's *Saint-Gaudens and the Gilded Era*; for artistic context, a general reader can look in the art section of any decent bookstore for titles about the beaux-arts sensibility, the work of Saint-Gaudens and Maxfield Parrish, or the architecture of Stanford White. I personally think the best way to understand the sculptor is to stand in front of his work and imagine what it might be like to make something like that.

Circular Reasoning: There are lots of books on dowsing, and lots of other books and articles that set out to prove that dowsing is bogus, and never the twain shall meet—as with the readings available on Mormons, much of what you see is biased. The story of Captain Thunderbolt is in general, low-level circulation around Vermont and appears in Dana Lee Goodman's *Vermont Saints and Sinners*; a brief recap of the story is also on the sign at the schoolhouse in Brookline. Background on the construction of the Round Church came from an issue of *The Vermonter* from 1933, in which Leonard Twynham writes about the concept of community churches and focuses specifically on the church in Richmond. The walking of labyrinths as a spiritual exercise is an ancient practice, and outdoor labyrinths are found in France, Scandinavia, Finland, Great Britain, and Estonia. There are labyrinths embedded in the floors of the cathedrals at Chartres, Amiens, and Reims, and in the Grace Episcopal Cathedral in San Francisco.

Border Lands: For background on Fenianism, I made good use of Wilfried Neidhardt's *Fenianism in North America*; the Vermont Historical Society also holds a privately printed book by Robert Magee called *The Fenian Raids*, composed from the Canadian perspective. The larger story of the Irish diaspora and the Irish struggle for autonomy has been written about extensively, and there has been a general surge of interest in Irish culture in the past several years, making materials even more abundant. I particularly like Kerby Miller and Paul Wagner's *Out of Ireland* because I am a sucker for good pictures, and relied on Peter Gray's *The Irish Famine* for pretty much the same reasons. The essay here also drew on contemporary newspaper accounts and on personal experience with the site—my trademark method throughout this book.

THIS IS NOT A WORK OF SCHOLARSHIP, and my impulse to cite even these background sources is grounded in the idea that nonscholars still feel the grip of curiosity, and curiosity should be honored. And encouraged, especially when it begins as idle and then moves into the higher gears. It's fun to know a few things, however sloppily the knowledge is acquired—every new piece of information we tinker with encourages future tinkering. Tinkering, as a human activity, is basically good: It can slow the heart and raise the mood and improve the dinner conversation, and I am old-fashioned enough to think people should talk over meals and not watch television. My point, if I have one, is that it is not necessary to be a scholar to pry into things, and if my cheerful methods rub off on a few readers who subsequently slip the leash on their own, so much the better.

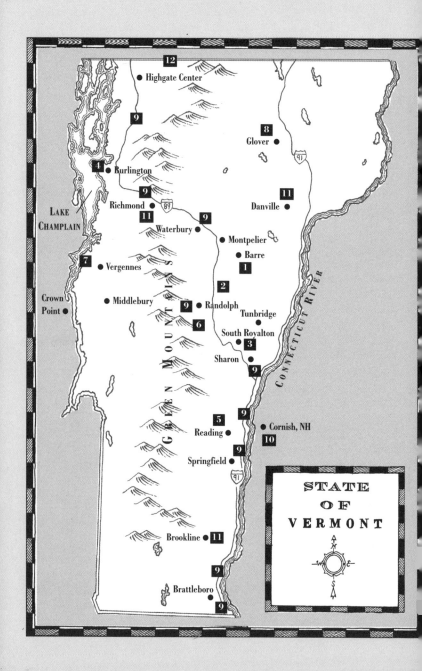